MW00354256

Bible

Interpretations

Fourteenth Series
October 7 – December 30, 1894

Matthew, Mark, Luke, Isaiah

Bible Interpretations

Fourteenth Series

Matthew, Mark, Luke, Isaiah

These Bible Interpretations were published in the Inter-Ocean Newspaper in Chicago, Illinois during the late eighteen nineties.

By

Emma Curtis Hopkins

President of the Emma Curtis Hopkins Theological Seminary at Chicago, Illinois

WISEWOMAN PRESS

Bible Interpretations: Fourteenth Series

By Emma Curtis Hopkins

Managing Editor: Michael Terranova

ISBN: 978-0945385-64-6

WiseWoman Press

Vancouver, WA 98665

www.wisewomanpress.com

www.emmacurtishopkins.com

CONTENTS

Editors Note

All lessons starting with the Seventh Series of Bible Interpretations will be Sunday postings from the Inter-Ocean Newspaper in Chicago, Illinois. Many of the lessons in the following series were retrieved from the International New Thought Association Archives, in Mesa, Arizona by, Rev Joanna Rogers. Many others were retrieved from libraries in Chicago, and the Library of Congress, by Rev. Natalie Jean.

All the lessons follow the Sunday School Lesson Plan published in "Peloubet's International Sunday School Lessons". The passages to be studied are selected by an International Committee of traditional Bible Scholars.

Some of the Emma's lessons don't have a title. In these cases the heading will say "Comments and Explanations of the Golden Text," followed by the Bible passages to be studied.

Foreword

By Rev. Natalie R. Jean

I have read many teachings by Emma Curtis Hopkins, but the teachings that touch the very essence of my soul are her Bible Interpretations. There are many books written on the teachings of the Bible, but none can touch the surface of the true messages more than these Bible interpretations. With each word you can feel and see how Spirit spoke through Emma. The mystical interpretations take you on a wonderful journey to Self Realization.

Each passage opens your consciousness to a new awareness of the realities of life. The illusions of life seem to disappear through each interpretation. Emma teaches that we are the key that unlocks the doorway to the light that shines within. She incorporates ideals of other religions into her teachings, in order to understand the commonalities, so that there is a complete understanding of our Oneness. Emma opens our eyes and mind to a better today and exciting future.

Emma Curtis Hopkins, one of the Founders of New Thought teaches us to love ourselves, to speak our Truth, and to focus on our Good. My life has moved in wonderful directions because of her teachings. I know the only thing that can move me in this world is God. May these interpretations guide you to a similar path and may you truly remember that "There Is Good For You and You Ought to Have It."

Introduction

Emma Curtis Hopkins was born in 1849 in Killingsly, Connecticut. She passed on April 8, 1925. Mrs. Hopkins had a marvelous education and could read many of the worlds classical texts in their original language. During her extensive studies she was always able to discover the Universal Truths in each of the world's sacred traditions. She quotes from many of these teachings in her writings. As she was a very private person, we know little about her personal life. What we do know has been gleaned from other people or from the archived writings we have been able to discover.

Emma Curtis Hopkins was one of the greatest influences on the New Thought movement in the United States. She taught over 50,000 people the Universal Truth of knowing "God is All there is." She taught many of founders of early New Thought, and in turn these individuals expanded the influence of her teachings. All of her writings encourage the student to enter into a personal relationship with God. She presses us to deny anything except the Truth of this spiritual Presence in every area of our lives. This is the central focus of all her teachings.

The first six series of Bible Interpretations were presented at her seminary in Chicago, Illinois. The remaining Series', probably close to thirty, were printed in the Inter Ocean Newspaper in Chicago. Many of the lessons are no longer available for various reasons. It is the intention of WiseWoman Press to publish as many of these Bible Interpretations as possible. Our hope is that any missing lessons will be found or directed to us.

I am very honored to join the long line of people that have been involved in publishing Emma Curtis Hopkins's Bible Interpretations. Some confusion exists as to the numbering sequence of the lessons. In the early 1920's many of the lessons were published by the Highwatch Fellowship. Inadvertently the first two lessons were omitted from the numbering system. Rev. Joanna Rogers has corrected this mistake by finding the first two lessons and restoring them to their rightful place in the order. Rev. Rogers has been able to find many of the missing lessons at the International New Thought Alliance archives in Mesa, Arizona. Rev. Rogers painstakingly scoured the archives for the missing lessons as well as for Mrs. Hopkins other works. She has published much of what was discovered. WiseWoman Press is now publishing the correctly numbered series of the Bible Interpretations.

In the early 1940's, there was a resurgence of interest in Emma's works. At that time, Highwatch Fellowship began to publish many of her writings, and it was then that *High Mysticism*, her seminal work was published. Previously, the material contained in High Mysticism was only available as individual lessons and was brought together in book form for the first time. Although there were many errors in these first publications and many Bible verses were incorrectly quoted, I am happy to announce that WiseWoman Press is now publishing *High Mysticism* in the a corrected format. This corrected form was scanned faithfully from the original, individual lessons.

The next person to publish some of the Bible Lessons was Rev. Marge Flotron from the Ministry of Truth International in Chicago, Illinois. She published the Bible Lessons as well as many of Emma's other works. By her initiative, Emma's writings were brought to a larger audience when DeVorss & Company, a longtime publisher of Truth Teachings, took on the publication of her key works.

In addition, Dr. Carmelita Trowbridge, founding minister of The Sanctuary of Truth in Alhambra, California, inspired her assistant minister, Rev. Shirley Lawrence, to publish many of Emma's works, including the first three series of Bible Interpretations. Rev. Lawrence created mail order courses for many of these Series. She has graciously passed on any information she had, in order to assure that these works continue to inspire individuals and groups who are called to further study of the teachings of Mrs. Hopkins.

Finally, a very special acknowledgement goes to Rev Natalie Jean, who has worked diligently to retrieve several of Emma's lessons from the Library of Congress, as well as libraries in Chicago. Rev. Jean hand-typed many of the lessons she found on microfilm. Much of what she found is on her website, www.highwatch.net.

It is with a grateful heart that I am able to pass on these wonderful teachings. I have been studying dear Emma's works for fifteen years. I was introduced to her writings by my mentor and teacher, Rev. Marcia Sutton. I have been overjoyed with the results of delving deeply into these Truth Teachings.

In 2004, I wrote a Sacred Covenant entitled "Resurrecting Emma," and created a website, www.emmacurtishopkins.com. The result of creating this covenant and website has brought many of Emma's works into my hands and has deepened my faith in God. As a result of my love for these works, I was led to become a member of Wise-Woman Press and to publish these wonderful teachings. God is Good.

My understanding of Truth from these divinely inspired teachings keeps bringing great Joy, Freedom, and Peace to my life.

Dear reader; It is with an open heart that I offer these works to you, and I know they will touch you as they have touched me. Together we are living in the Truth that God is truly present, and living for and through each of us.

The greatest Truth Emma presented to us is "My Good is my God, Omnipresent, Omnipotent and Omniscient."

Rev. Michael Terranova

WiseWoman Press

Vancouver, Washington, 2010

LESSON I

Jesus At Nazareth

Luke 4:16-30

There is an invisible musician forever near the keys of our being. He gets frightened sometimes and touches not the responding notes of our brains, or our eyes, or our ears; he gets an imagination that our brains, our eyes, our ears are not good enough for him to use, and then we complain of being weak-minded, blind, or deaf. That invisible musician who falters and fails is the human ego. It is the lord of the health and the beauty of the body.

It is each man's "my lord." It is not the Supreme One, the Highest the "Lord." It is that lord or manager of flesh and its ways which is ever and forever dealing with good and evil, right and wrong, happiness, and unhappiness, deafness and hearing, blindness and seeing, all the "pairs of opposites" that the theosophists tell of.

1

Jesus taught this human ego to listen to the supreme and unspeakable One, to the terrible Ego that knows nothing of the pairs of opposites, the Lord of Lords, the King of Kings.

Jesus gave today's esoteric philosophy in this text: *"The Lord said unto my Lord, Sit thou on my right hand till I make thine enemies thy footstool."* So, the invisible musician, whose name is lord of life, health and happiness, must declare himself on the right hand of the pairs of opposites. He must choose fearlessness where he is fright stricken; he must declare that my ears are as good as anybody's ears, cochlea, mailers, incus, and every other part, when he feels that they are not quite up to his wishes. Likewise of my brain and my teeth. Thus the lord or human ego is obedient to the first lesson of the Highest, or Superhuman Ego.

Jesus Teaches Uprightness

Whomever comes among us showing us a good method of attention to the highest, the superhuman, is a Jesus Christ. Wherever a Jesus Christ arises he tells of the right hand and the pairs of opposites continually. He says that if we know that a man is upright we can trust to the esoteric strength of his uprightness to legislate for our empire, kingdom, or republic, through him, in wisdom, prosperity, safety, not considering the matter of astuteness, acumen, shrewdness at all;

2

the upright man will pray the nation buoyantly over the seas of hierarchy, foreign enmity, personal understanding, and not a hair of our people's heads shall be hurt. He has no admiration whatever for political smartness, coupled with wine bibbing and adultery.

There must always be anarchy, poverty, private riches, and public poverty where such sitting on the left hand of the pairs of opposites is indulged in.

It is true that whoever looks toward the highest discovers that the highest, the Supreme One, whom Jesus Christ calls the "Lord," knows nothing of the pair of opposites. God is too pure to behold iniquity and all our righteousness is filthy rags of nothingness before and under him, but whoever is able to say "my head," or "my money," or "my hands," he is still talking and dealing with the creations and feelings and the world of the human ego, who is all mixed up if he doesn't stick to his right side of things till the wrong side of them gets under feet and out of sight.

The Pompous Claim of a Teacher

The invisible musician, the human ego, is a pathetic weather vane. Here comes a pompous claim of a teacher telling him that my ears need crutches, my feet need braces, my brain needs phosphorus, and the ego hurries to obey that teacher. Then along comes a teacher telling him that there are no ears to be crutched, no feet to walk with, no brain to play on, and the willing little ego agrees to that dogma. His teacher tells him that it is the most wonderful doctrine that ever came to the world, and if anybody disputes it let him anathematize all who proclaim that he uses ears; eyes, brains, or feet. He does not always have to tell aloud that he has no brains. His neighbors are convinced of that without his open avowal thereof, but concerning his eyes and ears he is most ardent to tell that he has none because his teacher said so.

But the -willing little ego, the invisible musician, has one command only from Jesus Christ mind. It is: "Sit thou on the right" of all questions, steadily, faithfully, till the wrong is under feet.

There is no direction to anathematize, none to hate, none to quarrel, none to call names, but one to stand for the right side in speech, thought, writings, conduct, till the wrong is by the Lord put under the feet. The human mind or lord over the body has no power to put death or anarchy under feet. The human mind or lord of the body has power only to sit on the good side of all questions.

When a human ego says that man is born to trouble he is on the left hand of the question of God's peace to man. The right hand is that the Highest Lord, knowing nothing of trouble, creating none, sends no trouble to any man. The human eye that says your brain is not a good one to use is on the left hand of the question of wisdom. The right hand of the question to sit on is that the Highest God is no respecter of spots where his wondrous wisdom dwells. The moment you tell that human ego, that invisible musician who is presiding over the keynotes of your brain, that your brain is as good as anybody's Socrates, Jesus, or Sakyamani not excepted, he will change his tactics toward you. If he has been thoroughly terror-stricken by some such left-hand dogma as that your brain is too old to pray on any more; you may have to talk reassuringly to him for many days before he will consent to the eternal truth that the Highest Brahm never sends old age. That world is a left-hand statement, a goat to be cast away.

Christian Science as it was reasoned out in the second book of "Christian Science," was the clarion call of the first esoteric lesson of Jesus, *"Sit thou on the right."* That book taught that "matter is the unreal, spirit is the real. Good is the only presence." This was sitting on the right of the question of substance. Its tendency was to put matter under feet. When Jesus, the boy carpenter, found that matter was under his feet he said he was able to put his body out of sight or bring it into sight.

Coomra Sami put the Himalaya Mountains out of sight by understanding the unreality of matter. The Christian Scientists put odious dwellings out of sight by sitting on the right hand of the question of substance. If they fail we know it is because matter seems real to them. The human ego, or invisible musician, whose business it is to deal with twos, or pairs of opposites finds himself handling an old brain with splendid skill, when he listens to the Jesus Christ principles. Did not Peter entrance thousands with the elixir of his spirit when he was in years terribly old? How could he do that except by taking the right hand of the question of spirit?

The Supreme One No Respecter of Persons

The musician who plays on the keynotes of your eyes ought to be told that your eyes are as good as any eyes. Jesus', Gautama's, Peter's not excepted. The Highest One as the human ego feels the warmth and beauty of when he looks toward the truth of him.

Wherever the young Jesus might have learned this law makes no difference; at 31 years of age he was master of the world by the understanding of it: "And he came to Nazareth, where he had been brought up, and, as his custom was, he went into the synagogue on the Sabbath day and stood up for to read." (Luke 4, 16-30)

"No matter if you are a Nazarene if you know the esoteric principles with your human ego the divine influences will attend you. Nazareth was a contemptible place in the estimation of people in the time of Jesus. It was not supposed that from that worn-out spot any brilliancy could arise. But the worn-out eye, ear, foot, brain, touched by the spiritually taught invisible musician, can see, hear, spring, electrify a globe.

The human ego, turning its listening mind toward the right, catches the songs of new life, new light, and the old instruments it has discarded as useless give forth music such as the ears of man have never heard before. And so Nazareth-poor, old, gray-haired, toothless brainless, blind city rose on the wings of a boy's love of the right and the good to be the glorious demonstration if what life is stirring near where the eyes seem dead and the brain useless.

The Great Awakening

And so the tired old globe, touched with the signals of decrepitude, springs up with a new smile when the boy's voice sounds on its ego's ears over the ages of misunderstanding of one of the simplest lessons of God to man:

"On airs from the hills of glory blow;

Oh life from the swells of the infinite flow

Let thy truth, my Father, descend upon me,

Let thy spirit, my Father, the whole world to see."

Nazareth means that branch of world science which treats of old age (De Senectute). When the science of God is brought to the ego and the ego agrees unto it there is no longer any such branch of instruction in our schools or pulpits. Nazareth stands for poverty of every sort. Old age is poverty of every sort. World science has taught the invisible musician who plays upon the keys of your being that you shall get poorer and poorer in sight, hearing, walking, thinking, till you have nothing but, dry dust to represent you on this earth; but spiritual science says that your sight, hearing, thinking, shall quicken, brighten, beautify, till the earth shall be filled with the ransomed who have forgotten world science through understanding God science.

"The spirit of the Lord is upon me, because he hath anointed me to preach the gospel to the poor; he hath sent me to heal the broken-hearted, to preach deliverance to the captives and recovering of sight to the blind, to set at liberty them that are bruised."

The Glory of God Will Come Back

Tell this news to the invisible musician, whose terror-stricken fingers have refused to play upon any part of your being. With this Jesus Christ Gospel the human ego will turn his weather vane attention and your spirit will return unto you as the glory of God returned unto Nazareth and stood

up with the beauty and ardor of the irresistible
Jesus.

Again and again has the light of eternal God
shone on the weather vane called human ego, asking it to agree with one side only of all the
questions up for discussion on the boards of human existence. And again and again has the
human ego of each man agreed with the left hand
of all questions, rushing out upon the Jesus Christ
man who has said that with the right is unchanging wisdom, absolute good. In verse 29 of this
object lesson we are told that Nazareth attempted
to throw Jesus down the hill to destroy him, but he
escaped alive.

The invisible musician whose business it shall
always be to deal with your affairs can take you
down hill if he listens to the left hand doctrines of
this world. He can take you up the mountain of
happiness if he listens to the right hand doctrines
taught by the spirit.

Listening to the spirit, he will never hear that
you are less than God, in your faculties. Listening
to the spirit he will never hear that you can faint
or fail. Listening to the spirit, he will never hear
that you are born to die. And when the ego that
handles your eyes and brain learns how wonderful
is the spirit, how different from matter, how wonderful is the science of Jesus Christ, so different
from the science of the present church and school,

he will sit on the right hand of sciences till he is Jesus Christ in power.

And then, as Jesus Christ, he is no longer human. He throws off the robe of human nature. He knows it is not robbery to be equal with God. By listening to the Highest he is the Highest. We are always that unto which we listen. We are identified with what we agree with. *"He that is identified with me sits in my throne,"*

Inter-Ocean Newspaper, October 7,1894

LESSON II

The Draught Of Fishes

Luke 5:1-11

That nation which has the greatest gold and silver resources must dictate the money metal of this planet. If England can show that her hills and mines are the richest of all the earth in gold and silver, she shall dictate bimetal or monumental. If Ceylon can show that the Lord hath thrown up greatest hills of silver and planted deepest beds of gold within her borders she may tell the world about money. For since time immemorial the buying and selling medium has been silver and gold. It is not the men who own most land in Russia who dictate policies but the men who own most gold and silver. It is not the men who own most land in our Republic who run us but the men who own most gold and silver.

In Joseph's time silver was more precious than gold. The Egyptians dictated that policy. They

could be independent about it, because they manu-
factured their own clothes and raised their own
grains. It was down into Egypt that Jacob must
send for his supplies in time of famine; it is down
into the country where gold and silver are found
most plentiful, which can be provided for within
her own borders and export in richest abundance,
that all other countries must go for information
about values.

This is illustrated by today's object lesson: *"He
taught them as one having authority."* Why? Because he owned the gold and silver, the cattle also,
and the creatures of the deep. He could make his
own clothes from their lamb and silkworm crudity
to their woven cloth usefulness.

To the fishers who had toiled all night under
dictations of authority that resulted in starvation
and discouragement he said: *"Strike out for your-
selves."* Do what the other four thousand ships
want to do but dare not do. I am aboard your ship
of State. I am he that proclaimeth the one principle only that has potency within itself to deal
justly and righteously with all men when a nation
agrees to it. If you agree that all human beings are
born with equal rights, independent of color, race,
sex, or ancestry, you have an irresistible principle.
Nothing pitted against it can stand. Even if you
tell those ships of war to sail to one side for you to
occupy their deep waters they shall obey, for I own
the most riches through having the most power-

fully operative principles, and therefore I am master. The setting-free principles are ever outwardly indicated by immense natural resources."

This interpretation is easily made from the parable of the freeing principle in the ship of misfortune. (Luke 5:1-11)

Launch out into the deep and let down your nets for a draught. And Simon, answering, said unto him, "Master, we have toiled all the night and have taken nothing, nevertheless as thy word I will let down the net."

The Protestant Within Every Man

There is one within every man that protests against pretty nearly every thing that goes on upon this earth. Do you not protest against a world arrangement whereby the man who overreaches his neighbor to the greatest extent is the greatest man in his community?

That protestant within you is the Jesus Christ quality within you. Do you not protest against getting $1 per day for doing your most honorable best while your employer gets $1,000 per day for the same struggle? That protestant within you is your Jesus Christ quality. He would overturn and overturn and overturn till he had things his own way if you would give up the reins of management into his hands by saying sometimes to him: "Have your own way with me." As, "At thy word, Master, I will let down my net."

Last Sunday's principle was illustrated by Nazareth, and its attempt to hurl Jesus Christ down a steep place to dash him to pieces. The fact that Nazareth means old age with its contemptible appearances and conditions, and Jesus Christ means protest against world measurements, shows that the protest against effeteness, senility, decrepitude, which people feel, is their Jesus Christ quality, to which they ought to say: "Have your own way." But instead of this, what has the prince of this world taught the decrepit to say: "I must go the way of all the earth. I must not expect to overturn the ordinances of nature."

What would the interior protestant to all this tell men of themselves if they would not hear his voice?

"Thy flesh shall be fresher as a child's, that thou shall return to the days of thy youth." Job 25)

Today's principle is illustrated by Capernaum, Lake Gennesareth. Capernaum means consolation, Gennesareth means completed. The fishermen had toiled all night for their living in the usual fashion but nothing had come of it. They were discouraged with misfortune. At this point in a man's career let him realize that his Jesus Christ quality speaks very plainly. He must change his policy. He must do what it seems impossible for him to do. At that point in the nations career when the mighty men are perished out of the land and the reins of state are in the hands of weakness, the poverty of the masses is great, the Jesus Christ voice that is raised in its midst is the people's voice. They are best brought forward in judgment and wisdom when their rulers are weakest. They own the silver and the gold, the fields and the seas. It is their mind which understands that their word may dictate the values, the standards, the policies on the sea of human ideas where ships of war, merchantmen, and common fishermen are struggling for authority.

The Cry of Those Who Suffer

Jesus Christ always rides in the ship of state with the laboring men and women, for they pray most. They have occasion to pray most. Therefore a nameless wisdom sits at the helm of their efforts. Let no man who has listened unto the prince of this world and got great wealth by any of the modern methods suppose that by building chapels and monasteries he can buy that nameless wisdom to ride in his affairs which makes the word law to the nations in that day when the circuit of misfortune is closing. The consolation of authoritative wisdom is with the poor.

"Vainly we offer each ample oblation,

Vainly with gifts would his favor secure.

Richer by far is the heart's adoration.

Dearer to God are the prayers of the poor."

From what ranks comes the love of freedom? From those who are most bound, of course. That love of Freedom is the Jesus Christ in man. From what ranks rises the most ardent prayer for assistance? From the most unfortunate, of course. That ardent prayer is the Jesus Christ in man. From what ranks rises the petition for rest? From tired and overworked, of course. That prayer for rest is the Jesus Christ in man. From what ranks rises the most sincere prayer for wisdom? From those who have made the greatest mistakes, of course. If the people, the lowliest, the enslaved to unremitting circumstances, have been those whose prayers have been most genuine, since the flower thereof has risen from the mud and rock of hardships, theirs is the boat on the waters of a nation's misfortune which holds the Jesus Christ man of authority, and nothing can resist their dictation on the silver and the gold question, the tariff and free-trade question the corporation and the labor question, when they give it.

This Bible lesson exposes the absolute certainty that the common people who have toiled all night with their country, but have taken nothing, shall make no mistake when they dictate terms to a globe on those questions which the other ships of state would like to do. When the circuit of misfortune closes for those who have realized most the beauty of freedom, believed most in divine assistance in calamity and ignominy, only they have the voice of Jesus Christ audibly speaking among them. His voice is lost amid the clanking chains of other men's fears of losing their riches, fears of losing their office, fears of being refused the old-time chances of syndicating the mines of coal, the stores of gold, the fields of copper, the grassy praises, which were spread forth for equal distribution among that people whose main principle is universal freedom.

Who realizes best what freedom of opportunity means? Who so well as those whose cry for a fair chance, for a helping hand is coldly slighted by their more favored sisters and brothers? Their realization of equal rights is the living presence of Jesus Christ. When they speak in the fullness of time their voice shall be obeyed.

<u>The Promise of Good Held in the Future</u>

There need be no fear of the people making any mistake when their circuit of misfortune is closed. They are at Capernaum, the consolation city. The long hour of the dominion of the favorites of the prince of this world passeth away as the shade of the night that can never return. *"They shall forget misery as waters that pass away."* (Verse 6)

It is a well-known principle in metaphysics that realization is demonstration. Every time a great truth is appreciated by you the appreciation is unvaryingly certain to demonstrate somehow. Jesus Christ realized that active movement of health through his being. He found that it worked its miracle instantaneously. The beggar child looking in at your plate glass window sees the bright grate, the white carpet, the pink china, the gold spoons, the yellow cakes, and is lost in speechless adoration. She forgets her own misery in enchanted realization of glories she has never shared in. The least of the animals in that white and gold room is above her in comfortableness, but which of you is Jesus Christ? Truly it is the one whose realization is most alive. Which brings out a home for something homeless, a meal for something hungry, a cloak for something cold, if realization is demonstration?

This is a homely and coarse and sordid and commonplace illustration. Maybe you would like to be told of one who should fall in a speechless enchantment of realization of Brahm, the absolute and changeless god, as Jonathan Edwards fell on the banks of the Connecticut River. What would be the results of his realization of unsearchable splendors? John says: "It doth not yet appear what we shall be," but Jonathan Edwards has been called the greatest thinker New England ever produced, because he is the only New Englander who ever lost himself in a trance of realization of the presence of the Unspeakable One. The glad effect of this same recognition was told by Sakya Muni in these words: "Oh, thou unshaken One, by thy favor my delusion is destroyed." Paul said he was less than the least of the saints, but this realization of the unsearchable riches of Christ gave the whole world a taste of the grace of God. Looking into the windows of the white palace of the eternal God, he, like the beggar child, less than the cat on your hearth rug, had realization. And realization is Jesus Christ.

Where the Living Christ is Found

He who hath realization hath the living Christ. Therefore the beggar child lost in enchanted sight. Paul, lost in enchanted sight; the fishermen lost in wonder (Verse 9), may show you who are today the living presence of Jesus Christ among us, whether you in your palace, cars and diamond necklace, whining because your neighbors furs are handsomer than yours, or the millions who, in their shivering hunger, are speaking to the God of supply till they are lost in enchanted adoration of his unsearchable riches.

When Munkacsy's "Christ before Pilate" was exhibited in Chicago the little fighting newsboys sobbed with adoration of that one whose unspeakable gentleness cause the proud and learned of the world to hang him on the cross.

"And the light and song of story

Gathered around his head sublime."

Their realization was the living Christ risen and speaking in Chicago. Whatever is spoken by one thus lost in realization is so authoritative that a globe full feels the thrill thereof. Run the gamut of your descriptions of the undescribable one from the high note of realization of the untold splendors of its abyssal dark to the lowly story of the awed adoration of the convicts in prison, who drew their hands back lest they contaminate the woman who had told them of the love of God, your highest righteousness is filthy rags (Verse 8), your lowest righteousness is no less; the fact forever stands that realization of good is the Jesus Christ in man; protest against injustice, unequal opportunities is the Jesus Christ in man; enchanted ecstasy of gladness that there is one who is not approached in vain in the day of calamity, is the Jesus Christ in man and whichever one among you is utterly given up to the divine protest, the glad recognition of God, is that one who can speak with authority and even the winds and the sea obey him.

The Bible lessons that mention ships all refer to national states more especially. This one tells that country that has the freest principles that, as free principle is Jesus Christ, it is sure of being obeyed when it dictates to other nations on questions of international concern, because the Jesus

Christ in man or nation is the authoritative principle, irresistible, omnipotent majesty.

Inter-Ocean Newspaper, October 14, 1894

LESSON III

A Sabbath In Capernaum

Mark 1:21-54

Last Sunday's Bible lesson held the true information of where the divine authority is most sure to be exercised wisely and by whom it will be exercised and none can prevent it, in time of great national poverty. It held the true direction for each individual who has toiled along any line for a long time without success.

The Nation will find the Jesus Christ voice among the common people. *Vox populi vox Det* (The voice of the people is the voice of God). They will change the whole state of affairs by taking one bold hold of governmental matters prompted by the inner rising of the universal love of justice and equal rights.

The individual will find his man of authority rising when his discouragement is at its worst, prompted by his inner conviction that there is no reason whatsoever for honest, faithful effort going forever unprofitable, while he sees his neighbors on the same human sea arriving at something worth while with half the fidelity.

The inner conviction that rises and speaks in man is the authoritative energy. It is singular that school and church ethics, to say nothing of religious principle, have not brought out this point of life science with something like definiteness.

The pitiful poetry and the sacred-eyed prose that tell of martyred truth and martyrs for truth are not bringing out of the authoritative, triumphing, resistless God fact of life, by any manner of means. They are as barnacling to a ship of state or a man's destiny as rum shops and oil trusts.

The following is barnacle:

"Truth forever on the scaffold,

Wrong forever on the throne;

Yet within the shadow ever standeth God,

Keeping watch above his own.

I'd rather walk in the dark with him

Than walk alone in the light.

In his dreaming Francis Xavier cried out to the panorama of his future career as it was prophetically mapped out before him, with all its horror of suffering, weariness, hunger, thirst, storms to be battled, heathen rage, dangers, death: "Yet more, O God, yet more."

These quotations read well, but there is in every reader of them an interior wonder why, if God is so powerful, if he created these heathen, if he is so anxious to beat darkness and Satan, why he doesn't have the fight out and ended, why he created heathen and pietists to fight each other; why he lets truth and her speakers hang "forever on scaffolds."

That inner wonder is the omnipotent authoritative principle in your little son and daughter. Let them express that wonder. Answer them the deepest wish of your heart on the subject. Your deepest wish is that it were not so inevitably martyring to stand for the right. That deep wish has its affirmation. That affirmation is the terrible Jesus Christ. Did you ever speak it? It reads: *"The truth makes free."* It reads: *"I, truth, will give you a mouth and wisdom which no man shall be able to gainsay, nor resist."* It reads: *"My yoke is easy and my burden is light."* It reads: *"If men keep my sayings he shall never see death."* It reads: *"If a man follows me he is in the light."*

Why Martyrdom has Been a Possibility

But you say, "Did not Xavier actually suffer all that was prophesied for truth's sake? Do we not have a host of men walking on the white plains of our highest reverence because they were burned and chopped to death for truth's sake?"

Today's lesson will explain that they were chopped and scaffolded for their lies, not for their truths.

God is principle, not person. When men agonize over mathematical problems they might turn their hair white as wool and gnaw their teeth to sawdust with looking for the right answers all to no purpose if they did not tell the truth on their slates. So a John Rogers, a Guyon, a Julian and Felix, may stay in prison, burn alive, smallpox themselves past recognition if they decline the everlasting truth that *"As I live, Lord, I know the thoughts that I think toward you, thoughts of peace and not of evil, to bring you an expected end." "Trust ye in the Lord forever, for in the Lord Jehovah is everlasting strength. There shall not a hair of your head be injured."*

The men of history did not let their heart promptings talk. That silence made their scaffolds. Is there any honor of the Jesus Christ in me if I say I am willing to suffer poverty and lashing for his sake?

It is a fabrication of my school and church-taught self conceit, astray from that honest heart's query which I ought to express. No decent mother asks a grandchild to deny itself and suffer for her sake. The good mother shields her child. "As one whom his mother comforteth so will I comfort you, saith the Lord." This is truth. Whoever has seen the Jesus Christ in his own heart face to face has seen that the easiest, safest, most triumphant, most comfortable, healthiest, freest path he can walk is on the path of his own heart's truth concerning what God is and what God does.

It is not a question of who is good in outward conduct, it is a question of who faces the God in his own self and tells what that God is. Outward conduct is a significator of war between heart and dogmas. There is not one living who will find any respect written in his heart's blood for an Almighty One who stands still keeping careful watch when he ought to be stirring himself. Not one of us has a grain of adoration in our system for an Omnipotent Being who compels any creature to walk in lightless dungeons that he may be glorified. Now, why don't we say so? This is a saving truth starting up in our synagogues. It is our Jesus Christ. It is the heart truth.

If any man says that all my trials and tribulations are God's struggle to express his divine nature through me I must say that I think he is a very feeble disappointing sort of god who can't do as he wills in the twinkling of an eye just as I have heard he could. Such a bold launching out of my words would throw off the first layer of religious barnacles on my heart, and I should then speak the pure truth that would unclinch the next set of barnacles.

The Truth Inoculated in Today's Lesson

The final truth concerning the power of my inherent God would read this way: "Yea, before the day was I am he and there is none that can deliver out of my hand. I will work and who shall let it."

Today's lesson, as found in (Mark 1:21-34), is about the comfortableness, the health, the splendor of free heart acknowledgments on the subject of God.

It repeats the golden text of last Sunday: *"He spake as one that had authority, and not as the scribes."* It tells of Capernaum again, or the comfort that the free heart acknowledgments bring.

If I tell what my schools and ministers told me I am a scribe. The final result of being a scribe is found in these two verses, 23 and 24: "And there was a man in their synagogue with an unclean spirit, and he cried out, saying: *'Let us alone; what have we to do with thee, thou Jesus of Nazareth? Art thou come to destroy us? I know thee who thou art, the Holy One of God!'"*

The heart's prompting is so opposed to what we have been poetized and prosed into supposing that we either get into a fire pile like Rogers or insanity like this man. Naturally we cry out to ask why the omnipotent good acts so harshly. This is acknowledging first promptings. As a good scribe or obedient child of early instruction, we would not cry a lisp. We should pitifully snivel that the infinite goodness had ordained us unto our fiery pathway or our wild despair for his own glory.

The very first prompting is the very first movement of Jesus Christ. At the next cry we speak forth the unhinderable fact that the omnipotent good destroys hardship, not formulates it. It is the eternal hush of sorrow, fire, and dying to acknowledge that we do not honestly adore a God who hides behind a shadow while we fight it out alone; our confidence is only to be placed in God who walks up and fights for us according to our native demand.

This works instantly. It comforts unspeakably. It doesn't wait a moment to test our faith. Read verse 25 and 26; "And Jesus rebuked him, saying, *'Hold thy peace and come out of him;'* and the unclean spirit came out of him."

Then it tells how amazed the scribes and Pharisees will be, because acknowledging your heart's native way of thinking and stopping your general suppositions will make you free, energetic, wise, the very exhibition of Jesus Christ. Notice that the demoniac is not remembered. Only the free, glorious Jesus is talked of. So all our former nonsense about the weakness and slowness of struggling God will be forgotten, and only our God who never mentions wasting an instant, who is always a refuser of the praises of suffering for his sake, will be talked of. As it says here; "Immediately his fame spread throughout."

The Injustice of Vicarious Suffering

There is not a heart that sees any justice in suffering for the sake of one who is able to do everything for himself and for us too. That not seeing is your Jesus Christ prompting. Talk it out. That is the "word that is nigh thee even in thy mouth and in thy heart." "Who is blind like the servant in whom my soul delighteth?" Scream out your divine blindness, ye men of earth's synagogues. So shall your God arise with freedom on his beams.

This lesson takes us out of church and school and into home life and there shows, under the story of Peter's wife's mother, how the inner protest against repeating the false dogma of God's afflicting people to glorify himself by, works the healing truth into irresistible sight. Speak your disfavor of such a God. You feel it. Tell it. This throws off your fever of excitement in trying to be so good that the wonderful one won't choose you to glorify himself by.

The full truth is that there never was any glorification of anybody or anything by suffering. This truth is native to the heart, while the glorification by suffering is hated. This hate is Jesus Christ. The glorifying by sorrow idea has fathered and mothered our miseries. Speak up the hate. "If a man hate not his father and mother he is not worthy of me."

No wonder John said: *"Behold the lamb of God that taketh away the mistake of the world."* The hate principle is the Jesus Christ in man. Does any man live who does not hate the performance of a man trying to set himself up by hurting his neighbor? How lamblike the omnipotent hate that is Jesus Christ has reposed through the generations in home and school and church of man!

"But lo! the days are hastening on,

   By prophet bards foretold,

When with the ever circling years

   Comes round the age of gold.

When truth shall over all the earth

   Its final splendors fling,

   And the whole world ring out the song

   Which now the angels sing."

Inter-Ocean Newspaper October 21, 1894

LESSON IV

The Paralytic Healed

Mark 2: 1-12

The subject of this lesson is "The Paralytic Healed." It is a study in the cure of human fear by the radiation of the Jesus Christ quality of Kind. There are two ways of conducting my life as related to this world, that I am traveling through. One is by the principle of doing in Rome as the Romans do regardless of divine ethics, and the other is by taking the Jesus Christ stand and holding to it.

By doing in Rome as the Romans do I must enter the lists of contest, competition, fight hand to hand, mind to mind, speech to speech with other men and women, to see who will win the splendid honor of having grabbed most gold and most adulation at the close of his quarrelsome existence. This process is all under the arrangement of "the prince of this world," so called by a young peasant who pledged himself to live the straight contrary of it. He said boldly: *"The prince of this world cometh and findeth nothing in me."* This so angered the men who were running in the lists, with each other that they ordered him off the planet, and to this day they have kept the paralyzing motto entirely opposite to his principles that "Competition is the life of trade."

Whoever enters the lists to run for his bread and box of gold prize, is under the liability to, and expectation of, death. Whoever takes the stand of that young peasant has no running to do, quarrels with nobody, lays up no gold, finds a manna substance falling like snow flakes all around him forever, out of which he manufactures his unfading, ever-lasting clothing, his sweet, delightful food; he dies not, he fears not, he has no cause for paralysis, palsy, apoplexy, *"In the way of his righteousness is life, and in the pathway thereof there is no death."*

It is upon him that those who have run their minds and legs to death in the race of human endeavor call with wild beast yells, with panther clutches, when they have got worsted in the fray urged on all mankind by that "influential member" of universal society, "the pride of this world."

Systems of Religion and Philosophy

There have been many systems of religion and philosophy set up by poor, sprawling humanity, for the purpose of dethroning the prince who is sometimes called Satan and sometimes called the principle of evil. None of them seems to work his discomfiture equal to that one wherein he is called nobody and nothing. "Is there a Satan?" I ask of Martin Luther and he avers that there is one for he has seen him. "Is there a Satan?" I ask of Schopenhauer, and he answers me no, but there is a principle of evil for he has felt it. "Is there a principle of evil?" I ask of the straight representative of the latest device for ousting the paralyzing engine, and she answers me, "No."

The young peasant declared that the prince of this world was powerless. He pronounced the principle of evil as *non est*. An honest study of his principles will uncover this to a certainty.

As it is to his God, or quality, that all the world turns when day of defeat arrives, we have a book written for calling us all to get acquainted as early as possible with his quality before ever the apoplectic shock, or paralytic stroke, or whatever else the instigator of competitions is keeping in store for us, has called our race off. *"Acquaint now thyself with me and be at peace."*

This book states the Jesus Christ system and takes up illustrations of its efficiency. It took a Moses with 2,000,000 bond slaves and showed how the leader of a labor movement should comport himself and with what spirit he should be imbued before he would see the principle of equal opportunities prevail. It took a husbandman and caused him to hire some men who wanted work and pay them for their day's labor exactly what he paid some other men who had also wanted work but did not get into the field till nearly sundown, to show the principle of equalization of money on the basis of doing the best you can.

The Principle of Equalization

By the Jesus Christ system the little cash girls and boys who run and wait on me in the great store would receive an equal sum of money per day with the men who own the building, because they are doing the best they can under the circumstances.

"Who does the best his circumstance allows

Does well, acts nobly; angels could do no more?"

But by the system of the "prince of this world" those angels would get $2,000 per day to put in the bank, while the cash girls would not get enough to buy hot soup.

Whoever even takes the name, Jesus Christ, on his lips will find his mental quality getting into subconscious antagonisms every day of his existence. The Brahmins have one teaching in which we are all advised not to have anything to do with seraphic beings, not to speak to them, nor describe them, for we shall certainly be plunged into mental and human afflictions if we do. By which they mean that the seraphic realm that presses so close at our hands has a divine system of equality on all matters and by coming in contact with it through watching some of its happy denisons, we are more or less purified of this world's mottoes, but not enough purified to be independent of them.

"Break open, ye airs, closing thick on my sight;

Break, golden red gates of the morning;

There's something, me thinks, lying close to my touch,

That longs on my gaze to be dawning.

It was because of the misery of the remnants of a man's being after he had been partially divested of commercial methods, school methods, war policies, that Jesus advised all men to attend to the God quality he brought with all their mind, soul, strength, heart. Only so were they in this world an unmolested company.

The Little Rift In School Methods

A New York paper informs us that the government is about to establish a pycho department in a certain school. In this department the scholars are to spend a certain number of hours each day in writing down all the cheerful, happy things they can imagine. They will have to actually strain themselves sometimes, thereby exercising all their mind's strength to think up happy facts and fancies. The professor assures them that at a certain point in their practice a chemical change will occur in their bodies from head to foot. The government is by this admission making a slight crack in the scholastic wall that has been built up against some awfully unscholastic principles which are pressing like the great waters of the reservoir, and through the little crack so innocently made will speedily rush the utter downfall of all our present school methods. "The master and the scholar shall perish out of the land," for "they shall all know Me from the least unto the greatest."

For after letting the first trickle of the Jesus Christ quality in, it is only a question of minutes when the whole quality will prevail, *"By thy words, thou art justified."*

By it, these scholars will soon see that there is no principle of gloom only as they made one for themselves. They will see that there is no principle of ignorance only as they made one. They will see that they themselves have always been standing at headquarters and practicing Lord God. As Lord God, they have made all the deformities and miseries of their world. As Lord God they will repent that they have made man. They will stop the wheels of time. They will stop creating fools.

They will cease from studying to know things. They will know themselves. They will no longer regard themselves as seeking to become like God. They will see that at their own intelligent standing place they are supreme and need accept no artificial platforms.

Letting a young man into the secret of his own intelligence, power, and originality will cause him to stay at home at his own headquarters, and thereby the schools must be depopulated. He will see that what his professor is telling him is the professor's point of view. Aristides saw Aesculapius because he made an Aesculapius. The professor sees a rock because he made one in the same way exactly that Aristides made his friend. There is no rock there, no matter how enthusiastic the self-deluded professor may be. How long do you suppose a lad is going to study things that he had discovered have no existence or reality?

What Self-Knowledge Will Bring

When he discovers that his bones can be chemically changed by his own mind he will be likely to experiment with his own mind instead of with bones. When he finds that his world will appear or disappear according as he turns the slides on or off his own mind he will be likely to practice mental slides. He will soon laugh at a professor who tells him he is made of water and salt. He will laugh at a professor who has to eat lemons and sugar while lecturing in order to clear his throat. He will see that it is all true enough from their standpoint, but he denies the common sense of their standpoint. Their standpoint is miles away from the headquarters fact that man at his intelligence point is God and needs nothing but himself. He will soon be asking them to acknowledge that as they have originating powers they had better be using them more sensibly than in creating stones and weak throats. It was by ignoring his teachers standpoints, and turning back upon himself that Empedocles found himself exclaiming. *"I am God."*

It was by turning away from the nonsense of shifting phenomena that Thales became confident that back here somewhere is the Invariable One.

If I made gloom by not thinking of cheerful things; if I made cheer by not thinking of gloomy things, what an autocrat am I if soon I find that not only my body but my very world shifts at my swing. Am I not then at the very spot occupied by Jesus Christ, who one moment said, *"Depart from me I never knew you,"* and the next said, *"I love my enemies to death."* May I not do what I please with what I formulated? "I can lay down my body and I can take it up," and I am neither worse nor better for the practice. I Am what I Am, and no swinging of originating and destroying phenomena can alter me.

All this is taught in three 'ways today. One way is by cold metaphysics, or at its latest insistence as metaphysics it is called Christian Science. By this you will find yourself holding a set of principles, which outwardly you have no confirmation of to the extreme extant you could wish till by attention you arrive at the mental prowess of a Coomra Sami, who could erase the Himalayas from sight and keep them erased as long as he pleased.

Another way is by the illustrative method recorded in our Bible. The third is by the individual experiences, which have come forcing themselves upon people, as Berkeley, Edwards, Collier. We have been accustomed to thinking gloomily of our own individual experiences, and this has formulated palsy, stagnation, or paralysis of something or other. It is at this point the illustrative method touches mankind in today's lesson, as found in (Mark, 11:1-12).

The Meaning of the Story of Capernaum

It is Capernaum again. It is at a private house. A man is so determined to get out of the paralyzing race of trying to keep up with all the ideas of his professions, and get ahead of them in the race if possible, that he climbs upon top of the house and drops in through the roof at the feet of one who never ran in the race of life because he knew himself and how to deal with himself.

The Jesus Christ man turned the paralytic's mental slide, and the exhausted creature saw that it was a mistake to suppose that any man must take any other man's estimates of him. He even saw that he need not keep his own estimate of himself.

Capernaum is a comfortable science to know, Capernaum means comfort. A private house means every man's own mind. Within his mind, at its heart's center, is his everlasting intelligence, full of healing of his hurt.

That central intelligence in man is his Jesus Christ. Let him not imagine that it is a feeble and timid quality that has to be coddled and praised. It is a rugged, hardy, unkillable energy. It was what Job hit hard blasphemous knocks without hurting it when he reasoned with the Almighty till he arose on the roof of his house and let himself down at its shining feet, conquering adversity and men's

41

learned arguments. Job had no friends like the
paralytic mentioned by Mark. We have the support of Edwards, Berkeley, Collier, Jesus, on our
metaphysical ascents, but like Job and this man
we must face our own intelligence before we are
independent.

Each man of us is of a palsied state while we
lie down upon the estimates placed upon ourselves
by other than the true inward soul. The bid of
false estimates is the bid of fear forever. The Jesus
Christ intelligence gives every man living, black or
white, male or female, the ability to see the world
from an undeluded standpoint.

In Verse 7 we find the wall of scholasticism
calling this blasphemy. But in verses 10 and 11 we
find how utterly indifferent to the scholastic views
of morals and manners that young man is who
knows that other men's attainments are only their
elected standpoints of solid delusions. The young
man turns the slide of the so-called sinner's mind
and shows him himself as he is. (Verses 5 and 11)

Immediately he is able to take up his bed and
go his way to his own house. Thus does any man
who turns the slide, which has deluded him into
agreeing with what is the common opinion concerning the world's substance and liabilities and
what is his business in the world.

He discovers that he has always been what he really is at his intelligence point, and may make up a cheerful estimate of himself or a gloomy one at his pleasure, as Jesus of Nazareth likened himself to a defeated hen one moment and crowned himself king of men and worlds the next without altering his eternal "I AM".

After this, we hear no more of the palsy man. We hear only of the Jesus Christ man. From the Jesus Christ man we learn that the only Satan there is we originated, as Aristides originated Minerva. The only principle of evil there is we originated by swinging our mind like a censer in a church to gloomy themes or cheerful ones. The only palsy possible we originated by doing in Rome as the Romans do, or, in other words, supposing with our neighbors.

From Jesus Christ we find that the prince of this world is a supposition only. Men have one common supposition. They do not like their supposition. It tires them to death. They suppose in common that things and people have to be dealt with in business and in society after the race, fight and scramble methods. They suppose in common that they ought to be friendly but can't.

The terrible efforts of our preachers to make us friendly with each other give them the palsy, and they only show by such struggles that they are whirring the common supposition that pen and things and events are actual verities to be harmonized and reconciled, or paralyze themselves by antagonisms, when the phenomena of men, things, and events are but the outward presentations of each man's own agreement with a supposition.

"The world is my mental presentation," said Schopenhauer. Why then not see that even the principle of evil, which he called God, was also but his mental presentation? Why not see how infinitely, wonderfully supreme over even his mind was his Jesus Christ intelligence?

"There is in the actual only the God I." When this was spoken the palsy of the world arose in plain view and disappeared. (Verse 12) Men all saw God at their own head-quarters, and that one look disclosed to each the terrible fact that he was alone in his own world supposing and non-supposing, clothing himself and unclothing himself, making himself one of many, or none, at his will, making heavens beyond heavens or gloomy worlds below worlds. At this disclosure man pauses from God office of creating and, there is silence in heaven. With this disclosure the seventh day has arrived, *"On the seventh day God rested,"* and intelligence stands shining free from palsying supposition.

Inter-Ocean Newspaper October 28, 1894

LESSON V

Reading Of Sacred Books

Mark 2:23-28, Mark 3:1-5

The Romans had a proverb: "Beware of the man of one book." They proclaimed him a dangerous antagonist. There are secret springs in all the standard books, and the one who has chosen a favorite from among them and often read it over, has without fail pressed some of those secret springs and heard or felt mysterious promptings of power or wisdom. Evidently Jesus of Nazareth was entirely cognizant of the inspirations of the ancient Jews. He could quote from their historic lore, from their moral code, from their esoteric intentions.

There is something vitally affective in reading over and over the Jewish sacred books. Also there is in reading the Hindu sacred, books. We feel it in the Koran. We discover deep wells of our own if we study Shakespeare to the exclusion of other authors. The reason that the book lives is because it keeps hitting our secret springs with its own vital jets and because we keep hitting its secret springs with original renderings. A book lives because we are able to read out of it more than its Author was aware of. "He builded wiser than he knew."

Were not David and Solomon in exalted, states while writing the Psalms? Did they not transcend their daily character and conduct while inditing (composing) songs to the sure presence of God in the universe?

Much reading of our Bible caused a certain man's eyeballs to grow anew in his head after they had been surgically removed. Reading over and over some formulas caused the Ephesians of old to work startling miracles. They read the words for what they meant on the face of them. That was eternality. They caught mystic purposes back of the words; that was magic. Our Bible is a book of magic with twelve formulas for working out each man's life into mastery over nature and destiny and independence of gods and men. These formulas are put thousands of ways and illustrated by thousands of examples.

The Interior Qualities

On the surface the whole reading matter is one thing. Interiorly it is quite another thing. When the majority of the world catches from its interior qualities, the formulas will stand aside. The interior qualities will themselves pass on when realized often. "There is one other disclosure in this book of magic, beyond even the spiritual promptings and powers. Spirit is not the last and Supremest one. I must be poor in spirit, as poor in matter, to lord it over the Sabbath principle instituted by the spirit.

Man in moments when he is exalted out of eternal facts is spiritually inspired. Our metaphysicians are often exalted by thinking of the Spirit everywhere present. They work miracles while in these states. They institute regulations of conduct for each other, which are as implicitly obeyed, as were the Sabbath ordnances, which Moses gave the adoring Jews.

They have forbiddings and biddings. Coming from spiritually enchanted moments, they tell me what I may read and may not read, how far I may reason and how far I may not, and unless I am a Jesus Christ Mind, I shall as certainly be haltered by their spiritual ropes as if I were a horse in a barn.

To the very spiritually awake men who felt the divine sanctity mood, which our pulpit orders get into until their hearers mop the gold tiled church floors with mental awe of them, Jesus of Nazareth said: *"I Am Lord over your sanctity."*

The principle is set forth in (Mark 2:23-28, and 3:1-5.) He proved that he was as dominant over their sacred states of mind as over their sacred states of body. (Mark 3:5:5) It here remarks that he was angry and grieved at the conceitedness of sanctified states of mind. As he was Lord over anger and grief, it is evident; he used those ingredients to chemicalize*(Look at the end of this lesson for definition) their piety as coolly and deliberately as a chef would put saleratus and pepper into fermented soup. Spiritually, which sacredly punishes me for discovering God in my neighbor, no matter what his character may be, is fermented soup. Jesus put a large dose of mental abhorrence into the pious atmospheres, and since that time the Sabbath has been more palatable.

The Indwelling God

Every one present at this meeting understood that within himself was something unspeakably different from the best he had thought, something majestically better than his religion. For one divine moment he faced the unreligioned God of his own being. There is one spot in every being that needs no religion. It is the God spot. Ask yourself: "does God have a religion to hold himself in order with?" Jesus had asked himself that question till he had got entirely free from outer formality and free from spiritual exaltations that ordained it. He was all God.

Algazali, the Mohammedan, studied the stars at night. To his external sight they looked like money pieces. To his higher reasoning, they were other suns of worlds. He wondered deeply what they might be to his faculty that was neither reason nor eyesight. The Christian metaphysician sees his neighbor with his external eyes as a bunch of personality. With his higher reasoning he knows he is a Divine presence. With the deep wonder he realizes that his neighbor is indeed what his higher science has not named.

It is that which transcended reason that Jesus appealed to. It never has any words, *"They held their peace."*

If I watch money pieces intently, I shall secure money pieces, even if I watch the ones I do not own. The Hindu philosophy teaches this. If I watch spiritual reasonings I shall secure spirituality. The Jewish philosophy teaches this. If I watch the Supreme in myself and everywhere present, I shall secure my own Supreme. The Jesus Christ philosophy teaches this.

The supreme in man once seen keeps him still. Twice seen opens his lips. Thrice seen transfigures him with supremacy. We learn this from the silence of the men when Jesus touched their highest. Then they lost all consciousness, except their unity with the spoken words: *"Stretch forth thine hand."* Beyond that they lost consciousness of everything except their authoritative energy. We become aware of the nothingness of reason, the powerlessness of muscle, under the melting authority of the Lord over sanctity. Reason at its top sparkle ceases. Muscle at its Goliath blow does nothing. Jesus Christ is present.

What shall it profit me if I reason better than the world, and dash my contemporaries down commercial rocks, if I lose sight of the Jesus Christ in me?

<u>Weakness Of The Flesh</u>

The effect of watching money pieces has not been all that the most plethoric watchers could have wished. Their bones and hearts have withered under the process. Age has seized them just as their skill in clutching had made them famous. The church has loved them; but nothing in her higher reasonings at their most sacred eloquence has kept off the withering, nay the sublime dogmas of the church have not held their very preachers from putrefaction. (Verse 1 and 5) "There was a man in the synagogue with a withered hand . . . He grieved for their hardness of heart."

Capernaum is the science of spirit. It is a comfortable science to know. The preachers thereof have much power and are much self-satisfied. But the withering hand hardening is as apparent in watchers of sublime reasonings as in watchers of money pieces. Jacob and Isaac were too decrepit to continue to see or use their hands.

Christian reasoners tremble like aspen leaves for the same natural causes. There is no everlasting healing of human hurts by any other watching than by watching that which in man knows on a different plane from nature; pungent, penetrating, all-conquering.

The Bible calls this nature with which you are gifted, the Jesus Christ of you. While you are reasoning out your own side of the case as banana-seller, or your parishioners quake with admiration, this unconvinced nature of yours stands silent. While you heed it not, your hardening proceeds. While you are "buying and selling and printing and building" this unnoticed nature of yours is standing close. If you were to stop a moment, you would see that something about you never enters into your trades. That which enters not into your daily matters is your soul. In our Bible it is called Jesus Christ.

The Unfound Spring

When you notice it you will find that the religionists are just discovering that all that they have been talking about has not appealed to the one secret spot in them, which they want touched. When you turn to look at your nature that is not identified with even your family life, and cannot seem to be rallied with your best religious efforts, you may know that the preachers in their churches are also turning to watch their untouched spring. As it declares here in Verse 2, they all watched Him to see what he would do. They wanted to accuse that nature in them that was so unappealed to. We have always been taught that that one within us that was not pacified by religious teachings should be called our satanic nature. But lo! It is our God nature. Watching it the restless businessman, stood speechless. (Mark 3:3) Watching it the restless ministers of spiritual dogmas, stood voiceless. (Mark 3:4)

They prefigured our age. "The sun stands still on Gideon, and the moon in the valleys of Ajalon." All the religions of the world hold still. All the wheels of business wait. The end of the world has struck the conscious mind of man. We can never move or speak again, except from our Supreme, unidentified mystery, which the book of magic we call our Bible, in today's double-handed purpose, by two chapters, calls our newly recognized Jesus Christ.

November 4, 1894

* This information was compiled by Rev P. Joanna Rogers

Emma uses the word chemicalized many times in her works as from September 24th 1889 Hop-

kins Metaphysical Association   meeting Emma
says this:

"If the little woman will only smile and say
that the scientists over the country are showing
beautiful symptoms of coming harmony and general good will, she will help hurry that harmony
and good will among each other, which would
make the Holy Spirit descend over all the earth
with new powers and new conditions for us all.

But it took her good pupil Charles Fillmore in
his book Revealing Word to give us this fuller ex-
planation:

"It is a condition in the mind that is brought
about by the conflict that takes place when a high
spiritual realization contacts an old error state of
consciousness. The mind of man is constantly at
work, and this work results in the production of
thought forms. These thought forms assume individual definiteness. They take on personality,
which works out into the body. Whenever a new
spiritual idea is introduced into the mind some
negative belief is disturbed. It resists, with this
resistance comes more or less commotion in the
consciousness. This is called 'chemicalization' this
can be greatly modified or eliminated by putting
the mind in divine order through denial. If the
cleansing baptism of denial does not precede the
Holy Spirit's descent, there is conflict in the consciousness - the old error thoughts contend for

their place, refuse to go out, and a veritable war is the result. When the conscious mind has been put in order, (in harmony), the Holy Spirit descends with peace like a dove."

LESSON VI

Spiritual Executiveness

Mark 3:6-19

Today's lesson is a treatment for the quickening of spiritual executiveness. Last Sunday's lesson was a treatment for restoration from financial withering, which has been caused by religious sanctification.

It is only to the awakened metaphysician that it is absolutely plain how the business man's numbness of limbs has its encouragement in his admiration of the holy ardor of his religious instructor. The financier standing amid the religious preachings, which have no power to revive his withered or withering functions, has yet to learn that the odor of sanctity which he so adoringly gives his gold to support is a most unhealthy atmosphere for his mind and body.

He has to be shown that there is a nameless, unsatisfied region of him, which is not identified with high religious announcements any more than it is identified with his trading or his marrying. When he turns to notice that unidentified region, he is looking straight toward the healing Jesus Christ in himself. One look at it makes him speechless. The same with the pulpit orator. The first time he acknowledges that unsatisfied, unconvinced, unidentified region within himself, he is as silent as the financier. It is recorded of Confucius that when Lao Tzu told him to live more after the promptings of his own spirit than the teachings of men, he was so stunned that he spoke not aloud for three days.

Next, after noting that unconvinced, forever adverse region within themselves, men speak with authority in a new fashion. Thirdly, by simply watching that independent something within themselves, which at their happiest moments is not identified with what is transpiring, they discover that they have executive powers quite unspeakably above their mental ranges.

It is only by undistracted attention for a certain length of time that all this is demonstrated.

The Teaching Of The Soul

Time does not count to a man after he has sighted his own soul's law once. He feels that there is a way of living that he could be joyfully identified with. His mind does not define it. His speech does not express it. His soul has its own language, which he understands, and it lives in him. He does not have to try to live. He does not have to valiantly strive to throw aside his tobacco-chewing or anything else. His well watched soul does that for him.   And if he does not yet stop cheating and chewing, he has not yet seen his soul, for it always lifts a man's conduct and speech into reproachless purity to see face to face that something within him which is not mixed up with his studies, his buying, or his family life. *"Because I live ye shall live also."* (John 14:19)

That which is not mixed up is the Jesus Christ in man. It does not at all signify whether there was ever a Jesus of Nazareth. The main question is, "What will occur to me if I watch that terrible one in me who never is mixed up with anything I do!" Keep track of these lessons from Sunday to Sunday and they will show you what the everlasting, unchangeable declaration of inspiration has been on this subject.

Ages before Lao Tzu taught it in his one little book, ages before the Carpenter of Nazareth is historied to have lived it, we have found one and the same assurances:

"By thine own soul's law learn to live."

"No bad fame can hurt thee."

"No good fame can help thee."

"No weapon formed against thee can prosper."

"On thee death hath no power."

"Thou shalt lack for nothing."

"Thou, holdest the keys of heaven."

"The eternal God is thy refuge."

Today's lesson repeats that there is an un-named and unmanageable something in this universe. It has been called God, but the descrip-tions of it are so different and those who have described it seem to have so little pull on it to car-ry out confirmations of their descriptions that even the costermonger (A hawker of fruit or vegetables) smiles when you tell him your idea of it. Dickens made one of his poverty-prostrated wretches say that the clergymen who prayed to the mysterious something, "seemed mostly to be talkin' to their-selves."

The Executive Power Of The Mind

This section of the Jesus Christ illustrations is to be found in (Mark 3:6-19). It is intended to show that man's mind has twelve executive powers, which he, as head center, may put forth and con-trol his destiny with. His own head center is his unmixed and unmixable original identity. It is that indifferent one within him that, no matter how ardent he was in politics, love or religion, it

was never enlisted. He, man, has called it his unregenerate, Satanic nature, and he has ignored it,
covered it up, crucified, browbeat, prayed over it,
all to no purpose, generation in and generation
out.

This chapter calls it our God nature. These
verses show how we act when we have watched it
long enough for our twelve gates of power to begin
to open.

We begin to do mysterious things by unusual
methods. We do not speak or act from the discriminative mind. We do not discriminate between
good and evil. We bunch them together in one
crowd and exercise them on the training grounds
of human life as master of them both. This indifferent unidentified region, within us all alike, is
not mind, though it handles mind; it is not matter,
though it manages matter; it is not spirit, though
it blows through the spirit.

Mind discriminates between good and evil, and
either fights evil or cowers under to it. But this
"unregenerate" Jesus Christ chooses a Judas and a
John to manipulate the world with, as coolly as a
doctor chooses strychnine and celery to manipulate nerves with.

The more we watch this region that follows us
around, forever unconverted, forever unappeased,
the less mind we have; the less we act from fore-

thought and judgment. What earthly judgment did Jesus show in picking out those twelve men? What foresighted prudence of discriminative discernment? One of his chief dogmas was; *"Take no thought."* (Luke 12:22) One of his most splendid promises was: *"In such an hour as ye think not."* One of his proudest praises of himself was that in his humiliation of being unnoticed, ignored, slandered, spit upon, "his judgment was taken away."

Vanity of Discrimination

All this discriminative judgment, of which the intellect is so vain, is only its distinction between notions of good and evil. The Jesus Christ in me is not a respecter. Judas eats at my table, and I love him even while he is sanctimoniously averring that I am a freebooter and need hanging. If I am watching the Jesus Christ in me, the Judas and the John are equally useful. Neither harms me. Neither advantages me.

What can be more gloriously triumphant than this One?

"It lives in me in its strength and glory;

   It lives in me with its life divine.

By the light of its presence I read life's story.

And the key to the world is mine."

The main proposition of this central being of me that I have never managed is: *"Look unto me and be ye saved, all ye ends of the earth."* (Isaiah 45:22)

My mind is a sordid, silly thing. Therefore it is of the earth; earthy, even while I am telling you that you, being divine from first to last, have no pneumonia. What can be a more sordid business than healing the sick, even if you have discriminated in favor of words as more ethereal medicines than pills? What can be more sinful than preaching in a pulpit, even if you have discriminated in favor of good as the only reality? How can it be sinful? Because sin is mistaking. Choosing badly. We choose badly when we choose anything. The sharpest note of Jesus Christ was: *"Not my will, but thine, be done."* (Matthew 26:39)

This lesson teaches that there is such a thing as getting out of the clutches of good and evil and being utterly identified to the ends of our earth with the unregenerate, unconverted, unmanageable something that fears not evil, loves not good, uses both together, and shakes the earth from center to ethers with the end of time and fate.

Even the wrath of man shall praise him.

Truth Cannot Be Bought Off

Buy off my writing, speaking, watching this, and yet it will come forth. Scare me, praise my silence, but its Gabriel trump has once sounded.

The part of man that has not yet been converted is not his devil but his Christ. Let him, in the midst of his buying and selling, his banking and his begging, turn to look once, just once, at his majestic portion of being that is not mixed up with either his banking or his begging, his preaching or his stealing and, slowly or swiftly, the hinges of his golden gates of divine power begin to move.

This only needs to be written once and have only one reader of the writing thereof to begin the opening of the twelve-leaved gate:

"Swing inward ye gates of the future,

Swing outward ye gates of the past."

Who hath turned to face his unregenerate nature and known it as his divine soul? Who has ceased to discriminate between earthly states through steadfast watch of his all-conquering, indifferent, interior one? He shall suddenly arise on the morning beams of heavenly freedom, taking all mankind with him. Where beats the heart that will not secretly say that it knows of its unsatisfied region? Where sings not the heart when told, that watching that region is finding God?

"Put golden padlocks on truth's lips.

Be callous as ye will,

From heart to heart the whole world round

Leaps one electric thrill."

And Christ Was Still

People have often wondered why the Jesus Christ doctrine has been so slow, has permitted so many martyrs, has required such toilsome steadfastness. It has been to the shame of its preachers that the enlistment shout of its religion has been the same as the enlistment shout of rum: "I offer you cold and hunger, rags and death!" Crawford, the novelist, makes a noble Jewish lad be led to crucifixion for Christ's sake, while as in Nypatia we read: *"The still Christ looked on."*

Unmasterable executiveness attends upon keeping my eye on my central nature which has not heretofore been noticed.

What is the truth of the matter? This, a Christ which is not executive to keeping its promises, is not worth either dying or living for. "If this be treason, make the most of it." This lesson breathes it out. It sustains its note. It shows that a religion which will let me be under the wheel of misfortune in powerless subservience after promising me that I shall not even trip my feet on a stone, shall be hid from the scourge of the tongue and have no cause for mourning in divine understanding, is the silly fabrication of a strong intellect. This lesson shows me that I will find my Jesus Christ nature able to handle my executioners without my calling even their names. It shows me that my twelve powers begin to swing their splendors over my universe the day I boldly acknowledge my soul at its headquarters here, whose everlastingly unconverted state I have, by instruction of my religions, ignored.

The Same Effects For Right And Wrong

Those twelve powers were called by certain names to designate their demonstrations. We find them when circling around Jacob, called by one set of names, and when circling around Jesus by another set. We find them called by another set of names when circling around science. In science, they are statements of principle.

Of one thing we may be certain, and that is that they are all bogus incompetents till we strike the One who can use them to sound his nature forth with mastery, over Pharisees and Herodians. (Verse 7) That One can use them to put aside all the powers of mind. (Verses 11-15) He can use them to set aside disadvantages. See verses where it tells of their having been sons of some human father, which means that some of our twelve executive powers have heretofore been used to energize fabricated religions which had no Jesus Christ in them, as in all cases where a still and useless God lets children be martyred, in hope of a heaven to come, or in the cause of rum by increasing its use the more we thunder against it.

Thunder for religion, and thunder against rum; they both increase their adherents by thundering. (Verse 17) Used valiantly before ever we see Jesus Christ at all, but nothing to any purpose, as witness the increase in paupery while John has been thundering for religion, and the increase in drinking while James has been thundering against rum. (Verse 17)

The Unrecognized Splendor Of The Soul

Once turn toward thine own soul which, in its unrecognized splendor, stands on the mountain top of indifference to thunder, (Verse 13) and all thy golden gates of efficiency begin to swing outward for the shining beams of the sun of heaven to shine on earth.

What untold executiveness in the Jesus Christ whose gospel has been so carefully wrapped in napkins of theology for 1900 years! What undefeatable intentions spring forth when the Jesus Christ in pauper and king, one and inseparable now and forever, is found by pauper and king alike to be their everlastingly unenlisted region of being!

Who can stay the morning when its banners fling long their colors on an eastern sky?

Who can stay the dominion of thy royal soul when its recognized right of way is heralded by celestial notes that fly as new songs of God on airs that mind has no knowledge of and nostrils cannot breathe?

Sustain the note long on the subtle winds that bear it as joy to the world its Lord is come, because each man hath now faced up his own soul!

"The morn swings incense silver grey,

The night is past.

No priest, no church can bar its sway,

The night is past."

Inter-Ocean Newspaper November 11, 1894

LESSON VII

The Twelve Powers Of The Soul

Matthew 5:3-15

Last Sunday's lesson gave the names of the twelve genii [energies] enclosed behind the golden gates of every man's being. It was mentioned that the identity of man, his changeless soul, has been described in many fashions, and the twelve powers with which he is gifted have had many sets of names, but that none of them has the practical energy of the name Jesus Christ for the soul, and the names of the twelve disciples for the powers of the soul.

Not a Bible used on the globe gets away from the twelve law lessons of Moses and their spiritualization in the twelve gospel lessons of Jesus.

Often these interpretations seem to fly beyond the ranges of the twelve, but in fact they never do. The study of the divine in all things awakens far-reaching knowledge so that the commonest Bible sentences glow with celestial fires. Would you expect a student of mathematics to keep on forever within the four walls of the addition, subtraction, multiplication and division tables? Would not the free mathematician soon find —

$$(x + y)^2 = x^2 + 2xy + y^2$$

"That is not arithmetic," yells the keeper within the tables. "It is mathematics," responds the progressive calculator, and he drives on into quadratics, vaguely wondering what the four-table man is whimpering about.

Thus with the student of the soul. He finds directly that, though Krishna with his twelve men, was a good illustration of the true soul and its twelve gates, Jesus is better. Though Buddha, with his twelve listeners, was a good copy book, Jesus is better. Though Arthur and his twelve knights were fairly good hints, Jesus is transcendently superior. Though Charlemagne and his twelve paladins might have satisfied a struggling and gullible age, nothing bears the test of civilization like the Man who stood on Hattin heights and pushed through the open gates of his own soul, his twelve undefeatable powers. Nothing like Him, be he myth or historic person, who willingly represented in His own life that region of every man's being which was never enlisted into interest in anything he ever did.

68

The Divine Ego in Every One

What is that in the beggar which never begs? That is the Jesus Christ of him. What was that in you, which you gave not when you signed those marriage bonds? That was the Jesus Christ in you. What is that in the queen which is never identified with earthly royalty? That is the Jesus Christ in her.

What was that which was not born when you were born, has never been interested in anything you have done while you have been on this planet, and will not die when you lie down? This is the Jesus Christ in you. It is sometimes called the divine ego in you, sometimes called the divine soul of you, sometimes your deathless, changeless spirit.

"Never the spirit was born.

The spirit shall cease to be never.

Changeless the spirit remains,

Birthless and deathless forever."

When Jacob and his twelve sons are set before us by whom to explain our divinity and its energies, we detect interest in cattle and wives too strongly to inspire us with close attention. When Krishna, Buddha, Arthur, walk before us by whom to explain our divinity and its glories, we turn away from obvious signs of discriminative partialities. When Jesus speaks, we hear the absolute language of our never-world-enlisted soul: *"My kingdom is not of this world."* (John 18:36)

Thus to the church of, which caught the mystic secret of that Name, the wonderful Lost Word was promised and the eating of hidden principles never revealed except through realization of its meanings.

Thus, to the watcher of his own soul, the only name that acts like a key to identification with light on the path, is that one which was once charged with the splendors of revelation. Are not all names charged with something? Are not all writings charged with something? Read Dumas' works and openly receive the word that runs through the enchanting pages. Is it not "brains"?

Read Shakespeare with open mind and catch the word. It is "Judas." Why? Because there we find intellect at the height of human possibility explaining the passions, the loves, the hates, the foibles of human life, as the strength of life. With what masterly enchantment he would make us forget that it is the Jesus Christ in man that is all there is of man.

Intellect, when offered the statement that love conquers death and goodness confers changeless beauty, declines the statement because appearances have not exhibited that way. What a describer of appearances is the Judas genius! When the Jesus Christ is heard speaking, what saith He? — *"Judge not according to appearances."* (John 7:24)

Spiritual Better than Material Wealth

In today's lesson, the JUDAS genius is opened out with the divine intelligence that pure poverty of appearances is God. He who is poor in earthly things is all mind. The charitable teachings which caused me to give everything I had or could get hold of to my religion promised me wealth of mind or spirit in lieu thereof. But the Jesus Christ in me is as little interested in my mental and spiritual stores as in my bank account. To the Judas mind, first of all, the soul fire declares: *"Blessed are the poor in spirit."* (Verse 3) They are God. The whole of God they are.

Whatever teaches one that wealth of spirit is better than wealth of silver is as Judas-like in religion as Shakespeare is in ethics. I am to own and possess nothing.

Lao-Tzu taught that we must produce, but not possess. Possession is robbery. The high mathematics of Jesus Christ says that I must surrender my mighty spirit, its dauntless glory I must not hold. So I let the spirit blow where it listeth. I gloat not to be spiritual. I couldn't be free while holding on to the spirit with might and main.

Through the first gate, Judas — namely, my intellect — I let all that I know and all that has been taught me go free. I know nothing. "The wisdom of the schools is foolishness with God."

Through the second gate, my mourning gate, my love of sacrifice gate, my idea that I am meritorious in giving up, my missionary and reformer spirit of mind gate, my SIMON or hearkening to the doctrines of men gate, flows comfort, power for a universe, when only the soul voice is heard.

Watching the One in me that has never yet been interested in the world, because its kingdom is not of this world, I find that through the third gate of my being, the ownership of the world is mine through giving up the world and bowing my head for my soul to do all things and know all things. Its ways are not my ways; yet let them be done. That in me which is not identified with what I am doing, I give it its own way. This is THADDEUS. That was my love of praise characteristic. The Jesus Christ in me is above praise. When I feel the power of my Jesus Christ nature blowing its white winds through that disposition, I shall not be praised any more. No wonder the monks and nuns disfigured themselves to get rid of praise. They had a glimpse of that one in them that esteemeth not praise.

To be free from praise is the third power of Christ. We do not seek or try to care nothing for praise — watching the one in us that is not elated when we are applauded will accomplish it for us. *"Because I live ye shall live also."* (John 14:19) The management of this universe from spiritual zephyrs to molten centers is in the fingers of Him that can wisely praise. One who is seeking for favor cannot praise anything wisely. The supreme of meekness is seeking not commendation. (Verse 5)

The fourth power that is manifest through giving the unenlisted One in me full control is radiance of confidence in the new life that supplants my former life. Turning to watch the soul entirely overturns past conditions. It is the JAMES gate. He who supplants. Confidence in the excellence of the new is not forced — it forces. The former state of James was trying to do the best he could. Now he knows that all that he does is divinely well done. (Verse 6)

The fifth is THOMAS. Before we turned to watch our mysterious One that is not mixed up with our human life, this Thomas quality was the discretion of our speech and actions. We bow to this Thomas gate for the indiscreet to reign. The discretion of the world shut Melanchthon's lips, but when discretion was lost in Luther, the Protestant Church sprang its millions upon millions into view. So the most merciful one is the most indiscreet and least self-protective one, for over his foolish head the new dispensation rolls its merciful provisions. Thomas means twin. Exactly like the highest discretion. In view of the fact that the fool turns out to be God in being fool. The early church tried to show that we should certainly all become fools for Christ's sake, thus obtaining mercy for the whole race.

The sixth is MATTHEW. The gift of Jehovah. The sight purged of sights. Pure blindness to what is going on. Clear sight of what the reigning principle of life is. Principle, or the Absolute, confers all when once it is seen. Do you see that this very day, not a moment's waiting every clerk in the store ought to get equal daily pay with the owner of the store? Do you see that the miners who go down into the mines ought to share with the stockholders equally, on the basis of all doing up to the best they could? Do you see that if I think the South Sea islanders need teaching, I am robbing them of their good name, since God, at their center, is as truly God as at the center of Jesus Christ?

Then, if all this you see, your sight is pure. There is a promise here that he who sees these things through close contemplation of the One at his own center, who is not pleased when he gives to beggars as beggars — since the divine in the beggars is what he should give unto — shall certainly see God come rolling down the ways of men to overturn and overturn and overturn the systems that are based on the presumptions of inequalities among men. (Verse 8)

The Fallacy of Rebuke

The seventh is the peaceableness of BARTHOLOMEW. Whoever thinks reproof is his mission is most haughty when reproved. There is no evidence of seeing the central soul in yourself like your freedom from rebuking. Finding in the thief something to rebuke, you certainly cannot be seeing his unrebukeble heart's center. The only rebuker is he who questions you from the center of the prison of your criticism, asking, "When saw ye me in prison?"

Have you noticed how death or idiocy strikes those whose breath is full of accusations? Do you remember Cagliostro's pledge to honor and respect the principle that always touched those who tore the truth from their neighbors? Did he not say that its effect was death or idiocy? Why tremble before me, and spend hours in decrying against me, if I know that your heart's center is the living Jesus? I shall be safely housed as a child of God, because I feel the warm rush of the untouchable One in me, whose brightest activity is peace. {Verse 9)

The eighth is PHILIP. Lover of horses. The message through strength of character, gained by sight of divine principle, is found in this verse: *"Blessed are they which are persecuted for right-eousness' sake, for theirs is the kingdom of heaven."* (Verse 10) There is nothing like the love that flows from your strong heart when you feel this Philip gate open. The persecutions of men seem like children's toy soldiers. In symbology, horses stand for the swiftness and strength of any principle, which is plain to you.

The mother knows that her boy is good. Let her trust her knowledge. If the neighbors think he is bad, if the police are after him, never mind; her knowledge is the working factor. The neighbors will soon be proud to know him when he was young. Why trembleth the mother at opinions of others? Knowledge is a better working factor than are opinions. So with love. If you love anybody, why don't you trust that love to straighten out the tangles between you? Never mind what is interfering. Love is stronger than death or discord. Notice how it is here given that the kingdom of harmony is his who has felt the Christ in him as the strength of him. What Jesus Christ principle is plain to you? Keep your eye on it. It will give you a heart of oak. Stand to it. Swiftness and strength are in its legs. (Verse 10)

Andrew, the Unchanging One

The ninth is ANDREW. This gate of power being opened, the joy of the unchanging presence rushes through, Andrew is the unchanging one. To know that the presence of God in the universe is the extensiveness of your own soul is to find your own everywhere-present soul. Wherever you walk you meet yourself. What should it profit you to gain the friendship of mankind as the prince of this world, and lose sight of the spreading forth of your own divine essence? The day when you, by sight of God at your center, recognize that evil speech against you is truly a subtle breath of *elixir vitae*, you are opened on the Andrew side and can never feel pain any more. (Verse 11)

The tenth is JOHN. Grace of God. Three thousand times more than you could expect of mercifulness and graciousness. Every way you turn, rearward, forward, to right, to left, angels on angels working your miracles for you. Did you ever expect one blessing but have two instead? That was free grace. The thief on the cross asked only for one thought, and he got all heaven. This was free grace. Something wrought an easy victory for Jacob. That was free grace. How often Jesus taught that something would go before me, plead my cause and defend me. This is free grace. How much he said about my doing nothing, for something stood ready to break through my life with miracle-working in my behalf. This is free grace. (Verse 12)

The eleventh is JAMES, the son of Zebedee. That power which we have been exercising as an ambition we find being run through as beauty. Ambition is ashes. The promise is "beauty for ashes," *"Ye are the salt of the earth, but if the salt have lost its savor wherewith shall it be salted?"*

(Verse 13) This savorless life drops down. The salty savor that Elisha sweetened the brackish, tasteless lot of the theological students at Jericho with, makes beauty everywhere.

Notice that in this illustrative exercise the divine in man speaks through the last two gates with two overpowering assertions. Through the gate of falling ambition when the divine radiance streams in, it is plain that life is worth living. Ye are the salt, the beauty giver, the changeless wisdom of this universe.

"Ye are the light of the world. A city that is set on a hill cannot be hid." (Verse 14) This is the SIMON PETER gate. The light that streams because of blunders made. When you had been so steadily worldly wise that you were the wonder and admiration of your neighbors, what was that which caused you to undo the whole reputation at one stroke? That was your Simon Peter quality. Blunders enough, of that unexpected sort, would make a Jesus Christ light of you.

The Nameless Power In Man

Whose preaching was so brilliant that it converted 3,000 in one day? Simon Peter's. Who made more blunders than all the rest of the disciples put together? Simon Peter. What good did the blunders do? They caused him to see that if there were not some power and wisdom different from the power and wisdom of his human mind he would be utterly lost. Between speech and that nameless power, man has always interposed his mind. He has thought that if he would employ his mind constantly in training his affairs they would go well. He has believed that his thoughts could beautify or spoil his body. But affairs and body may be moved to more splendid achievements by recognizing that there is a nameless something — not mind — which is on the move when a blunder is made. Mind uses words; silent or audible words. But the kingdom of God is not in word but in power.

It was this power that Jesus had. It surrounded His words, filled them, enchanted them. "Never man spake like this man." Under its charm, the commonest words are miracle working. The blunders of life are overshone with splendor. The failures of life are divinely ablaze. Sir John Franklin's failure after failure made him famous. Thorwaldsen's failure married him to greatness.

"High over the plans and the schemes of men,

    the wills of the gods are decreeing."

It is not the gods, however, to whom the soul is looking, but to God. Ajax shook his clenched fist at the gods, and swore to escape in spite of them, but there is no escaping God. Let not man mention of God if he expect not God to act, for the mention of Him trips the feet and tongue. Especially does sighting the divine and telling his place undo the wisdom of a lifetime.

These, then, are the twelve plain influences that flow over our universe when we give dominion to that One within us who has never yet been identified with anything we have done. They are the subject of the Sermon on the Mount. The sight of a man of the description of Jesus is given to call our attention by an illustrative method to our own lofty nature. The twelve effects of recognizing the unenlisted lofty principles within us are found here in (Matthew 5:3-15.)

The Jesus Christ principle in us is not afraid of the intellect, never insults it, but uses it for different purposes than ordinary.

The Jesus Christ in us is the most terrible thing for us to look at. It will seem to be doing nothing after we have told it to have its own way, but what it is doing is beyond describing.

It melts the rocks of destiny. It stops the mouths of kings. Thrones totter. Ignored and unknown men and women take the reins of school and state. The more accurate the description of this central One with its twelve genii or energies, the more speedy and complete the changes in human affairs.

When a more accurate statement of the divinity of man than this is given, still more wonderful manifestations of the new age will be visible.

What mighty hand holds the globe so still? What unhearing One refuses man's petitions? What do the clouds of the night skies hide as men grope with furtive movements in this age that is shutting down its covers on the determination of every man to compete against every other man neck-and-neck, not to give most, but to get most?

Half way toward morning on Egypt's dark sands — how deep the night is! The mighty stars lie still on everlasting beds of black. But the night is not night to our soul. The stars of the dark are shining globes of untold light to that One within us whose eternal non-enlistment in earthly transactions has been our gloom, whose face being once seen, compels us to be not like Him, but all Him.

Inter-Ocean Newspaper November 18, 1894

LESSON VIII

Things Not Understood Attributed To Satan

Mark 3:22-35

There are certain students of pure mental action who have arrived at extraordinary mental abilities. They are able, by turning little cranks and cogs in your mind, to make you think you cannot hear common conversation. Then, by reversing the cranks and cogs, you can hear again.

On the mental plane, they are doing exactly what materialists do when they paralyze with cocaine, then stimulate with cocaine. One practice is a little more ethereal than the other; that is all. On that mental plane of performance, mistakes are apt to occur, as on the material plane accidents may happen.

When people are devoting themselves to performing on either of these planes, they are apt to decry the other plane. The less they know about the other plane, the louder their condemnations.

People who are very mental are praised very much for finding flaws in the Jesus Christ man who is managing affairs by a system that is neither mental nor material. *"He casteth out devils by Beelzebub."* (Verse 22) These are designated by Mark, who wrote an apologue of the soul, as "Scribes." "Scribes" in symbolic language, are mentalists. They deal with ideas.

On this purely mental plane, I aver (confirm), mistakes are liable. Coomra Sami, examining a noble-purposed European traveler, discovered that he had mental secrets, which composed a quality of character, which it would not flatter him much to have made known, either to himself or his friends. Now a man must be very strong-purposed indeed to hold his own in the midst of a set of "scribes" who have been dissecting his human mind and have pounced upon some mysterious cog in it, which they have named "Satan."

Mark speaks of one man, a carpenter's son, who was thus pounced upon by some mental scientists, or men and women who claimed to be great character readers. The way He held His own with them shows that the mysterious cog which they called Satan was equal to outdoing their most powerful Satan. He hushed them up completely by turning on them an argument *ad hornine* (to live), which, though not so stupendous in itself, since their own Socratic judgments could have adduced it (and probably did, secretly), was yet so charged with nameless fire, as from some unknown realm of terribleness, that immediately those great character readers slunk into shriveled fears lest they had offended God Himself.

True Meaning of Hatha Yoga

Christian Science, so called, began as the name of a process of transportation, with one William S. Adams, in the year 1844. He emphasised the hatha yoga practices of the recognized church of Christendom. What is "hatha yoga practice"? It is the proper name for all and every kind of physical operation for the purpose of being more heavenly minded. If you go without eating in order that you may be more mental or celestial, you are practicing "hatha yoga." If you give your money to a hospital to quiet your conscience for the number of times you took advantage of other business men, you are practicing "hatha yoga."

If you lock yourself into a room and throw the key out of the tenth-story window to keep yourself from stealing because you feel that you want to be moral, you are practicing "hatha yoga."

All signing of pledges and prohibition enact-
ments to train our boys out of handling wine
glasses so that they may be more God-like, are
"hathe yoga." It is a new name for such performances, to be sure, so far as we Occidentals are
concerned, but it is a very interesting name and
conveys the whole significance of church and phil-
anthropic forced conduct.

We have the history of Simeon, the Stylite,
carrying outward conduct to the extreme in the
hope of being more extremely heavenly. He
perched on a tower 60 feet high for 37 years, with
an iron chain about his neck which drew his fore-
head down to touch his feet. He believed that if we
do anything, we ought to do it with all our might.
He was practicing the presence of God by outward
deportment.

Mr. William S. Adams advocated strict outward deportment as a pathway into a heavenly
mind. He called it Christian Science.

The next type of performance for being more
seraphic was also called Christian Science. This
advocated thinking with the mind in certain described and prescribed fashions. At a certain state
of progress in this "raja yoga" practice, we were
discovered to be "scribes" almost equal to Coomra
Sami, the marvelous, for we found out Satans in
every body of people we met who differed from us,

or who disclosed to us turns of mind not declared to be the heritage of all in common.

Today's lesson handles us all without gloves. He who deals on the material, plane is not to be despised, but all the good he does is from the undescribed and undescribable miracle Presence which is not matter. (Verse 25) He who turns cranks and cogs in the human mind and there finds something bad to undo is not to be condemned, but all the good he accomplishes is by the inrushing of some mighty essential which is as different from mind as from matter, and which knows nothing whatever of the badness in matter or the badness in mind. (Verse 23)

The Superhuman Power Within Man

This lesson calls attention to the region in man, which knows nothing about his sickness no matter how bodily sick he may be. Hufeland discovered this indifferent region in his royal patients, and by steadfastly fixing his mind's eye on it; he brought a radiance from it through all the diseased parts of the body. Take notice that it was not by studying matter that he cured matter. It was not by detecting false ideas (mental equivalents) and pouncing upon them that he cured mind. It was by keeping his mind's eye on something in his patients, which had nothing to do with disease or error, body or mind.

The four Gospels in the Christian Bible are devoted to a skillful presentation of this region in all mankind. You have it, no matter how much badness you find in yourself, bodily or mentally. Today's lesson raps you hard on the head and knuckles to call your attention to the superhuman power you have in your Self, which is to be exhibited, not by practicing with detecting cancer spots and burning them out with material irons; not by finding flaws in character and singeing them out with sarcasms; but by being steadfastly watched as the one region in you which knows nothing about badness, but one shine of which on your pathway makes you the irresistible miracle of God.

In the four Gospels, this region in you is called "Jesus Christ". This is as good a name to call it by as the word "Principle," or "Soul," or "God," or "Absolute and Eternal One."

Paul, the student of both speculative philosophy and dogmatic theology, gave as his opinion that there is a kind of mental cataract over everybody's attention when called by any other name than "Jesus Christ." He detected that calling it by that name was followed by terrible upsettings of all kinds of human conditions. That name was really the new name, he said. It is the key to the "Lost Word," or the word that filleth the universe, yet is not now pronounced.

In today's lesson, that Man who once stood up and agreed to watch that indifferent region of His own being, and let it absolutely have its own way with Him, is again shown up as an undefeateble conqueror of all obstacles, mental, social, material, moral, religious, philosophic. (Verse 35)

The Problem of Living and Prospering

Now, if you are happy in your lot, dwelling in a state of lofty indifference to what happens, finding never anything to irritate or antagonize you, nor even anything which has power in itself over you to make you happy or glad, you have watched the Jesus Christ in yourself until you are all it. For this Man is represented as showing how easily He sets aside criticisms without feeling their stings, and how easily He sets aside love, praise, security of home, popular applause, as having no power over Him whatsoever. (Verses 30 & 35)

He demonstrates in His own life the power of God in man. It has now come to be an open question on this planet whether those principles of Jesus of Nazareth proclaimed 1900 years ago are livable. Can I — can anybody, without one single personal or intellectual advantage, actually drink from a fountain of splendor which will enable me to support myself without competing along any line or on any plane with my fellow beings?

This is what the four Gospels, marching a Jesus Christ throughout their message, aver not only can be done, but must be done or we all die of futile struggling.

This Man ran not in the race with any man. "Go in and win," we tell our young men. So they go in, neck-and-neck, like chariots in a Roman race. Most of them are finally broken up, undone. "The world has been one too many for me," whispered poor old Tulliver, who had "gone in to win."

Is there any way to live and prosper without trying my hand among human beings as if I were playing a game of cards — and without trumps or with them — for if I win not, I'm nobody?

If I'm an artist and I want my picture hung on a certain hook because it honestly belongs there, but the judge is one I must hocus pocus or bribe in order to get it there, is there a way to have my honest dues without playing that card of human ability, which I do not hold in my hand, since 1 know not how to hocus pocus, and I have no money? The four Gospels teach that I may and absolutely shall have my honest dues without holding in my hand or mind any card of human opportunity, right in the face and eyes of one who, side by side with me, both hocus pocuses the human judge, and handsomely bribes him besides.

Suffering Not Ordained For Good

As there is beautiful bodily healing sure to one who has learned how to see the wonderful spot in himself which never knew that he was sick; as there is untold wisdom of mind sure to one who has learned to see that wonderful spot in himself which never heard of foolishness; so there is security from human antagonisms, safety from human warfares, prosperity for every man, woman, child, right here on this planet, black or white, male or female, serf or prince, or the Gospels are a deceitful fabrication.

The Jesus Christ in men rises with irresistible grandeur when it is looked at and proclaims, "I will give you a mouth and wisdom which no man shall be able to gainsay or resist." This happens when the "scribes" of the world sit in judgment on thoughts and call that mysterious cog wheel with which no mind hath ever yet tampered safely "a Beelzebub." That fiery, untamable One in man, being given absolute sway, proclaims over the hills and plains of earth: *"They shall hunger no more, neither thirst any more; neither shall the sun light on them, nor any heat. For the Lamb which is in the midst of the throne shall feed them, shall lead them unto living fountains of waters: and God shall wipe away all tears from their eyes."* (Revelation 7:16-17)

91

Who is this that dares arise and proclaim that hunger and imprisonment, or competition with human beings for your living and your rights, are God-ordained methods for training you into safe pastures?

There's a Lamb in the midst of you. Look and live. He's the Lion of the Tribe of Judah, terrible as an army with banners in his awful defense of you, you poor defeated child of human instructions! Look and rest. *"I will contend with him that contendeth against thee."* (Isaiah 49:25)

Now, the question ought to be, not "Will the Jesus Christ principles work" but "Has anybody ever tried them?"

Did you ever know anybody who watched the Lamb in the midst of him till it rose and spread his table with plenty in the face and eyes of those who had stolen his money and his chances? Did you ever know anybody who had watched the Lamb in the midst of him till it rose and healed him of death in the face and eyes of those who had plunged at him with sabers or stolen his right to the true thought, namely, that life was his destiny and not death? Did you ever know of one who watched the Lamb in the midst of him till it came up as the stupendous ability to rise out of and away from the clenching determinations of family or daily obligations, or earthly king, to govern his notions?

The Lamb in the Midst Shall Lead

Was it an evidence of watching the Lamb for John Rogers to burn at the stake while his wife and babies looked on in weeping helplessness? Is it an evidence of your watching the Lamb in the midst of you till it rises as a Lion of might, which is the Gospel doctrine of "Lamb"; if you are poor, sick, misrepresented, cheated, gasping for breath, on the highway of struggle for your life and your knowledge of which way to turn? .

This is the will of God, namely, that you let the Lamb in the midst of you lead you. The "Lamb" is the Jesus Christ in you. The Jesus Christ in you is that region, that spot, that One, that still and un-described nature which shines through thoughts with miracle-working flames; which transfigures and transcends bodies with glistening health and beauty; which overturns the world for your sake.

Looking round on the upturned faces of a race that has been betrayed into supposing that to "go in and win" is the only way to arrive anywhere, it saith: *"Behold My mother and My brethren."* (Verse 34) Show I unto you a more excellent way. For your sakes, I close the books of time. For your sakes, My Kingdom is exposed on earth.

"Here death cannot reach us,

Where we have come:

Here naught can undo us;

God is our home."

This lesson teaches that there is no virtue in picking flaws. It is a waste of time, no matter on which plane we are practicing. The miracle moves on every plane, discriminating against neither. The miracle attendeth us at every stop of our way. Speculative philosophy is not worthwhile till it points to the Flawless One. Material science is not worthwhile till it finds the Flawless One whose every glance is a miracle of merciful kindness.

Where is this Flawless One? The four Gospels declare that with all His miracle-working splendor. He maketh His abode in you.

Inter-Ocean Newspaper November 25, 1894

LESSON IX

Independence Of Mind

Luke 7:24-35

Today's lesson is a metaphysical treatment for the independence of mind and character.

The claim of unworthiness is self-destruction. The true "I AM" within us never felt unworthy, and never said that It did in any way, shape or fashion. The true "I AM" may march you into the wilderness and keep you forty days without eating, or it may feed you sumptuously at kings' tables, but It is not a reed shaken by the winds of starvation or over-feeding, it is the independent One who can convert the sand grains into bread and kings' tables into clouds any instant.

When a man is in great poverty and owes for his board he is apt to think it is very religious in him to bow his reed-shaken head in that wind and say that it is the Lord's will. Then if he is made governor of money he again thinks himself very religious if he humbly thanks the giver of that state of affairs. That also is the Lord's will, he says.

Let him not be deceived. The "Son of Man is Lord" of the winds." (Luke 7:24-35) He that knoweth himself can help himself and that is the only Lord's will that there is.

The claim of unworthiness is the "John the Baptist" claim in religion and in philosophy. *"There cometh one after me the latchet of whose shoes I am not worthy to unloose."* Poor John. That killed him. That man would continually insist upon talking appearances. According to appearances, Carlyle averred we all ought to be hanged. That is true, but why judge by appearances? Why not spend all the days you once elected to devote to this planet, in speaking and judging from that other "I AM" in you, which never once admitted its unworthiness?

There is something about you that never bowed the head to any wind of adversity, and never swung as a victim to prosperity. It can wring the neck of adversity any moment, and set its heel on the swells of prosperity, Lord of them both with cool divinity. If you have felt how powerless you were to stem the tide of affairs you were judging as John, who was in prison and could not get out.

Was not the same authority seated in him that spoke so plainly in his cousin Jesus?

Who is this that saith a diamond though a very small one, is more precious in value than a rye straw? Is it Jesus or John? According to Jesus the sparrow, little inferior looking bird, without a particle of beauty or genius, is as charged with divinity as Princess Victoria Maude.

He That Knoweth Himself Is Enlightened

The doctrine of unworthiness is all very well for the judgment by outwards, said Jesus, (Luke 7:28) but the slightest admission that the authority of the indwelling soul is greater than the most powerful appearances, is more Godlike. (Verse 28) If there was ever a strong treatment for independence of mind and character, it is read forth from the verses selected for today's meditation. "Wisdom is justified of her children." "No bad fame can hurt thee, no good fame can help thee." Take that for a truth. At headquarters where thou art seated, no matter what thy name, where thou wast born or how much leverage on earthly chances thou hast, thou art what thou art, and who can, alter thee? "He that knoweth himself is enlightened," said the Chinese mystic; even before it was written over the Delphic temple. So long as thou thinkest it is the Lord's will that thou be subject to chances, not master thereof, thou art facing annihilation. But John's fate shows thee.

The instant thou knowest the kingdom of God, there is no death. (Verse 28)

There is no evil. There is no matter. There is no absence of life, substance or intelligence. There is nothing to hate. There is no sin, no sickness, no death. This is truth. Doth it so appear? How would you have me answer — from my Jesus standpoint, or my John standpoint? Would you have me imprison myself in Castle Macherus, beyond the Jordan, in self-destructive agreements with, outward claims, or liberate myself forever from sin, death end fate by the words of the Jesus Christ in me? One is the temporal, transient John "shadow that declineth" of me, while the other is from everlasting to everlasting, authority over outward claims, life, substance , and intelligence unanswerable, all powerful divinity.

The day hath now come when all men prefer to answer for their divinity standpoint, except the "Pharisees and lawyers". (Verse 30) "Pharisees" is a symbolic term for pious natures whose whole religion has consisted in ability to pick flaws. "Lawyers" is a symbolic term for literalists, or those who take the letter of the pious books for truth and do no thinking for themselves. Verse 29 declares that it is much easier for people who have always regarded themselves as unworthy reprobates to find their center of gravity, their divinity point, than for those who have laid great stress always on the inward sinfulness of their neighbors. "The patience and faith, of the saints," John wrote, were kept up because of expectation of self-piety being rewarded and neighbors' sins being punished.

The true "I AM" would have us all to know that it is not a reward for piety that authority over sin, death and fate is given to any man, but independent of his piety or his wickedness, his divinity is what it is as an independent esse. (to be)

The Universal Passion For Saving Souls

The swift allusion to people who feel that their own souls are saved, and now it is their duty to save others, as found in Verse 30 of this Chapter 7 of Luke, it is very sharp. No man's soul was ever saved. He never lost it. It was never in danger. Therefore it is nobody's business to go out and save souls. This verse explains that even the doctrine of unworthiness is more readily given up than this passion for saving souls. The passion for saving souls goes to very great lengths when given the lead to a man. The Puritans were so anxious to save souls that they burned their neighbors as witches. Mohammed was so anxious to save souls that his followers imitate him to this day by wearing swords while they are preaching, to decapitate anybody who disputes them. In every country there are great buildings, with thousands of pining wishers for freedom, shut up in them in the belief that their souls are better off.

They are dwelling and thinking and believing on the plane of insubstantial appearance. The treatment of the day's section is summed up in (Verse 35); "Wisdom is justified of her children." There is not one who is told of his independent divinity who sooner or later does not accept it. Then when one man in any city knows of that independent one in himself, he naturally turns to it in the day of being shaken in the wind of adversity, or even when housed in the King's favor. (Verses 24-25) Neither state is satisfactory, as all who have tried the ups and downs of outward life can testify.

As a man turns to examine his authoritative divinity within himself, he will feel himself rising in his majesty and proclaiming that his divinity is supremely independent of the circumstances that surround him. That crystal beauty of the mystic body, whose name in man is Christ Jesus, has a far reaching radiance of splendor to lighten the gentiles and glorify the pious. It needs no church, no school, no rostrum. Yet everywhere men will be found preaching boldly of their "I AM" nature. Everywhere men will be preaching boldly that the true Christ minister heals the sick by discovering the equal divinity in all mankind; sets the captive free by secretly whispering to them of their free divinity, opens deaf ears by noticing the unspoilable soul in all alike.

Wisdom is justified by the rapid spread of knowledge of the way to demonstrate freedom. John comes clothed in poverty, and is accused of having evil in him, but it toucheth not the fact of his being. Jesus comes eating and dressing comfortably, and it altereth him not at his center of gravity to be called a glutton. (Verses 25-34) Nothing whatsoever hath any power over one who has roused himself to proclaim that the divinity in him is the reality of him, and all that happens is nothing whatsoever to him.

Strength From Knowledge Of Self

The least among mankind with this knowledge in him is stronger than judges, stronger than juries, stronger than armies. The poor, the weak, the aged, the deaf, the blind, the defeated, and defrauded, let them be told of the unalterable, unlossable, divinity within themselves, that is able to shake off the flimsy rags of their seeming inferiorities and cause them to be strong, clear seeing, capable.

This is as definite a lesson for the student of mental action as for the student of externals. "The children of this generation" are those who are interested in metaphysics. Was there ever an age when the mystic, the metaphysician, the ideal, was so interesting to so many multitudes? But see, one gets afraid of opposing thoughts and falls at his post from what he calls the adverse thoughts of his foes. Now there are among these "children of this generation" of interest in things mystical, a certain number who know enough of the stately independence of their own divinity, never absent from them, to decline to laugh at the dictates of friendly thoughts when they feel them lighting on their minds. To decline to mourn when they feel the unkind criticism lavished on them from the thoughts of their contemporaries. They are as independent of unwritten and unheralded thoughts as of outward conditions. (Verse 32) *"We have piped unto you and ye have not danced; we have mourned unto you and ye have not wept."*

Outside of the metaphysics that particularly attends upon the "children of this generation," it is not taught that good thoughts flying through the airs make people who receive them happy, and bad thoughts flying through the airs make people unhappy, but it is one of the elementary insistences of modern psychics.

This man, whom Luke, the physician in Galilee nearly two thousand years ago, called up to represent the activity of the divinity in me, in you, in all alike, stands among the metaphysical teachings as unmoved by thoughts of their hearts as by speech of their lips or strike of their swords. In (Verse 32) he proclaims that no man's thoughts through the airs should please you by their cheerful commendation, and no man's thoughts through the airs should depress you.

The true "I AM is as independent of psychic forces as of guns and deafness.

Effect Of Mentally Directed Blows

The true "I AM" pipes and dances at nobody's tuning-up. Sublime in his standing place of knowledge of who he is, whence he is going, and what is his value, he is as naked of the rags of pleasant opinions and adverse judgments, mentally, as of physical circumstances.

In Utah they tell of one who fell dead from mentally directed criticisms. In Pennsylvania they tell of one who fell dead from mentally directed blows. In Boston they name several who were mentally discharged from this globe. In New York there is the same story. Now, let those who are of that reedy stuff, blowing down when savage winds strike them, lifting high when joyous praises reach them through the secret airs of silence, remember that the Jesus Christ in them is as utterly independent of secret thoughts that fly as of stones that are hurled openly.

"Thou shalt be hid from the scourge of the tongue." "Thou shalt not be afraid for the arrow that flyeth by day nor the pestilence that walketh in darkness."

The wonderful divinity within us all. "Who believed our report, or to whom hath the arm of the Lord been revealed?"

Independent of the rags of appearances, independent of the rags of opinions, naked of the shroud of human circumstances; naked of the shroud of human mind. Thus shineth not only this historic Jesus of Nazareth, standing free from the attacks of this universe, defying the attraction of gravitation, the drowning power of water, and the swaying power of psychologic forces, but the divinity in every child that asks you for crusts, and in your own self also, ready to bear you away on its bosom; Lord of life and death, master of things present and to come, free from the earth and the skies, independent of men and of angels.

"Cast all your care on God,

> *That anchor holds.*

Yea, in the uttermost stress of life's sea,

> *Calmly standeth the Christ of thee — free!"*

Inter-Ocean Newspaper December 2, 1894

LESSON X

The Gift Of Untaught Wisdom

Luke 8:4-15

Ingersol had discovered that the devil is not so powerful as the Lord, but he is quicker. That is true. The Lord being already here and everywhere forever, does not have to hurry up to get any-where, but the devil being nowhere had to scramble to try to be somewhere.

This is primarily the reasons why all scramble and struggle to be something or to own something or to do something are so unlike the changeless ever present One. Thus the Jesus Christ doctrine is explicitly one of statement of what already is; it also mentions what is not. And it all resides in assertions, which attend to their own business after they are uttered.

Whoever utters an assertion of any kind will see it walk close up to him in some event just like it. The central fire of our being does not have to think and plan in a smart, bright way to make up a set of logarithms or corner all the wheat in this republic. Being already all wise, already owning everything, it does not have to have brains to know what silver and gold to buy with.

It is very plain, then, that the more we are like the central fire of our being, the less we shall have to think in order to know, and the less we shall have to labor and grab in order to possess.

"The silver and the gold are already mine; and the cattle upon a thousand hills."

"I am understanding, I am strength."

Mohammed told his followers that they did not have to scream in order to make the Most Merciful One hear them, neither did they have to mumble secretly. He would hear them just as well if they talked in an ordinary tone of voice. As Mohammed stood with a drawn sword to cut off the heads of all who should dispute him, it was that impossible for them to talk to the Most Merciful One in an ordinary tone of voice that they to this day have shown only one effect of the assertion, that is the great number of believers in Mohammed.

The natural effect of the idea that a Most Merciful One is very near is to discover a friend and co-worker at every corner. *"Thou are the one"*, is what colorful address expresses. Not that the friend is thereby created, but exposed, for there is something about everybody that is very friendly to us. Once finding that something in him or her we rest easy. We are not afraid.

The Secret Of Good Comradeship

Today's lesson gives the secret of good friendship — comradeship. It is always the "they" who do not know anything. *"Unto you it is given to know."* (Verse 10) And as it is to everyone, everywhere, that the "you" is addressed, we finally wake up to discover that the "they" are nowhere.

"Unto you it is given to know." All the rest are stony, wayside sort of beings who never could know anything, never could own anything, and never had yet made their appearance in our society. This lesson is, therefore, a treatment for safe conduct over this planet.

As it is here expressly told us that unto us is the gift of knowledge, we may make the assertion boldly that we know all things and do not have to exercise any thought — shovels, hoes or metal reaping and thrashing machinery in order to know anything.

The most wonderful principle that has ever been known to man is the gift principle. Judas gave place to Matthias. Judas was intellect, thinking, planning, conniving, calculating, figuring. He split himself with good judgment, shrewd nineteenth century policy. "Business is business." "A man must make a living", said the cat to the canary, as he pulled him through the bars of the cage.

But Matthias, who takes the place of intellect, is the gift of the one who regardeth not my excellent figuring, who forgiveth (giveth for) my lost gold pieces, a treasure that cannot be lost. And over the highway of such a new manner of knowing, not a particle of judgment, discretion, foresight in it; over the head of the new fortune that taketh the place of my lost estates, shineth the giver.

There is a giver. A knower. You did not work with shovel and surgeon's knife and earn what is truly yours. You did not burn midnight oil over Sanskrit and conic sections to earn what you truly know. What you know you know, and what you own is yours without earning. If you seem to have land, stocks, elevators, by hard labor, can you take them along where you are planning to go never to return? Did you bring any of them with you when you came hither? Well, then, those are but symbols of the knowledge that is yours; symbols of the riches that are yours. The giver is not attending to symbols. He is entirely occupied in bestowing eternal, unchanging treasures.

The giver stands in every man. The knower stands in every man. It is my business to recognize that fact in spite of the evidence of my senses, and in spite of my shrewd penetration of character.

By Luke, the giver and knower standing up in myself, is called Jesus Christ. He tells me to assert the knower and giver in you instantly when I see you. The rest of the world know nothing and own nothing so far as I am concerned. You are all in all. *"Ye are the light of the world."* By thus addressing you I shall thus behold you. If I address you by describing you as fickle, wayside soil as mentioned in (Verse 12), that is the way I shall always see you. But this lesson says it is not "you", ever, who are fickle, it is "they". This giver in me always gives you credit for knowing everything, owning everything, and giving thirty, sixty, one hundred times more than I spoke to about as necessary, when I was calculating intellectually how much you ought to give. (Verse 15) Mark tells the proportion, he discovered people always contributed to you wherever you gave them credit for knowing all things. The lessons in these gospels are all meant to be interpreted by Matthias, and not by Judas. That is, by the sudden gift of untaught wisdom and not by the intellect.

"He that hath ears to hear let him hear."

By the sudden gift of untaught wisdom I know that if I undertake to explain some of you as filled with the cares and riches of this world I shall be explaining you through intellect. That intellect of mine would keep me doctoring you for diseases, cutting off your legs, teaching you free trade or protection, change of Presidents, and salvation of souls round and round like a windmill age in and age out.

The gift of untaught wisdom would cause me to see you as awake in unspoilable health of body and everlasting soundness of limbs. It would see you as knowing that no Judas policy of dealing with political issues forever will amount to prosperity for mankind.

A man, 70-odd years old had been afflicted with asthma in worst form for many years. One day he suddenly threw his mind away with the despairing request that the invisible Lord would help him. Suddenly he was cured, and though that was more than three years ago, he has never had the slightest return of asthmatic symptoms since. He declares that his faith in the Lord is so precious to him that he would not on any account use a material symbol as a remedy. The Lord, the everywhere present Reality, always shall be his healer. He was about to address a labor organization, urging free trade as a remedy for adversity, when someone told him that the Lord was as much the prosperity for mankind as their health.

Laying Down The Symbols

How could he preach symbols to people when neither the symbol called free trade, nor the one called protection, nor eight-hour, nor greenback, nor antitrust had in it, so long as the global revolves any healing of adversity?

Having laid down one set of symbols he could easily lay down his dependence on the other set.

Do you think audiences of men and women are not able to bear being told to stop expecting any healing of their hurts through different politics, one way today, another tomorrow, through steady politics, changeless dynasty or good measure, because only by the Lord can they ever be prospered?

If you think this way you will split. See (Acts 1 & 18.) For you are calculating on men as a Judas. It is the "they" who are destroyed. The "you" being your audience will bear the most unreasonable, improbable, unbelievable propositions, so long as you address that in them, which is the Knower, the Owner and the Giver. Take a position, with all the people you meet, that this lesson defines, and you will find friends everywhere, generous givers everywhere. In you they will find a wise friend, a generous giver. This is the position: *"Unto you it is given to know the mysteries of the Kingdom of God."* (Verse 10) The "you" and the "they" are the

111

subject of this address, and the "you" are everywhere. The "they" are not visible. They never will be.

By this sudden wreckage of intellect, the gift of a new knowledge of men is vouchsafed. Addressing you as knower of all the mysteries of God, owners of all the riches of the kingdom, I feel myself in wonderful company! Where is that evil set of people who are engrossed with ungodly ways of jumping in and out of banks and pulpits, factories and ships, hurrying up and down, getting the better of each other or the worst of each other, swifter than a weaver's shuttle in their movements, while "you" abide in majestic calm, possessed already of all knowledge and all riches? According to this lesson, nowhere. "You" are all that live.

"You" do not have to chew symbols called pills and sulphur, in order to be what you are. "You" do not have to dig and delve, write and set up type for your prosperity. These are the things that "they" see, who, seeing, see not, and hearing hear not. "They" are the dead. Let the dead go on burying dead, marrying, sailing, wrangling, but "you" never do these things, "You" know all things. "You" being already in calm possession of all that is, do not have to be quick about what you do else go under, either to adversity or accident.

Intellect The Devil Which Misleads

This lesson teaches that there is no reality in the intellect. Poor intellect; it has had the running of all outward things for many generations, but it hasn't arrived anywhere worthwhile. It is furbished up so it now shineth like polished steel, it is quick as lightning in skipping from pillar to post, but it never has any story to tell, only the grave and my ignorance and wickedness; and it has no directions on my journey only for me to be on hand and scrabble to die.

The intellect is what Ingersoll means by his devil, "who is not powerful, but quick". For it is the intellect that speedily built those splendid buildings and calculated that the men who carried the mortar up to the seventeenth story ought not to share equally with those who sat in their offices and planned where the money should come form; and then said the whole of them must die.

It is the intellect that figures "you" up as of different grades of intelligence. But the Jesus Christ sees "you" as the union of all knowledge. When we interpret the gospel lessons intellectually, seeing the ways of men that are not present, we are overcome with gloom to think how slowly the good moves; how much bloodshed and disappointment it has let go on age in and age out. When we discover that such interpretations are what make slowness, powerlessness and disappointment hide the "you" everywhere we will not use them.

Luke addresses his books to "Theophilus", which means to the God chord in you. He makes one man stand up and see the Knower in you, and nothing else; the Owner in you, and nothing else. He makes this man face "you" everywhere and face nobody else. He says that there really is nothing anywhere only the knower standing up in you and the Owner standing up in you. Those who know nothing and own nothing are absent.

Luke would show me that not only does the sparkling divinity, the majestic Jesus Christ, stand up in me, but in "you" also and there is no-body for me to reckon with forever and ever only "you the wonderful.

Interpretation Of The Day's Lesson

Luke makes Jesus Christ in me speak in an ordinary calm, conversational tone to "you". I do not carry a drawn sword of any ability to hurt you if you refuse to be called wonderful — wonderful because the Knower in me knows that you love to be told how wonderful "you" are, while "they" know nothing and never will know anything.

If the Judas interpretation is given I shall be obliged to tell you that you are a lot of fishermen who cannot, some of you, even write your names, and you have no social position whatsoever, which are outward signs that I should keep out of sight of you. Luke's Jesus Christ did not trim his speech or conduct to catch the "best people", while "those" who interpret intellectually, to this day, beam with pious triumph if "their" audiences are Rothchilds, Chesterfields and Carlyles.

The Matthias interpretation takes now, with today's lesson its place in this world.

"You" are the Knowers; "You" are the "light" the "salt"; the shining presence of beauty and power and "You" are everywhere."

This assertion attends to its own business. The principle of assertion is the Jesus Christ prerogative. If I make you to remember the look of my human face, all you can remember will be my best in character and motive. If I make the assertion that unto you is given to know all things, I shall soon be unable to find a fool among you. If I say that unto you be given divine ownership I shall soon be unable to find lack anywhere.

Inter-Ocean Newspaper December 9, 1894

LESSON XI

The Divine Eye Within

Matthew 5:5-16

There is a book entitled "Magia Jesu Christi." It has this lesson of today in it, and explains Matthew as telling in an esoteric humor how every man may learn to strike out for himself and defeat the universal conspiracy against him. The best of it is that he is not to hurt or cheat, or connive or contrive; he is not to have a solitary external advantage, yet the vary devils of destiny and human unfriendliness are to curl down and disappear wherever he arrives. (Matt. 5:16)

There is one impartial will that liveth and dieth not, and in that will all that which ought to be is.

All trying to set up wills to have things better or worse than they seem to be, is veiling the city of splendor that lies before us, close at our hand.

There, in that city that really lieth so near us, all that which ought to be, already is. Matthew discovered that the Jesus Christ in man is continually giving a message to the different natures in man. That message is; "Exercise no human will. By it thou makest a veil. Cease from willing and thou shalt see the kingdom in which all that which ought to be is". *"I came not"*, said the offspring of David, *to do mine own will, but the will of him that sent me." "The kingdom of heaven is at hand."* (Verse 7)

There have always been two standpoints to view our surroundings from. One is from the veiled standpoint and the other the unveiled. With the sight clear we see things in heavenly order. With the sight veiled we are miserably dissatisfied. The moment we have our own human will we begin to feel the teeth of the artificial wolves. (Verse 16) When we see from the divine eye within us we are the wolves and everything feels our teeth.

The divine eye within us, seeing things in its own fashion, asketh us to give up seeing things any other way but its way. That divine eye is called Jesus Christ by Matthew. It is a single eye. Our double-eyed state stands for our double standpoints, double-mindedness, two-willed human estate, whereby we see into Samaria one moment and get entangled among the gentiles the next. (Verse 5)

The Jesus Christ in us sees no artificial goodness; that is, goodness forced before our faces by the strong wills of certain men who have lived on this planet. The civilization of this age is Samaria. It is artificial excellence. It is nothing but a make-believe. It is a veil cast over against the presence of the real city, *"Go ye into the city of the people of Israel."* (Verse 6)

Knowledge Which Prevails Over Civilization

"Israel" means prevailed over civilization and the strong-willed Greeks that are forcing more of it before our faces. Now and then, you do find sane people who do not think that it was ever meant that we should get our strength by eating oxen. They believe that strength is a seeing faculty. They do not think that knowledge is attained by mental eating. They feel that knowing is seeing with the single eye. Go and associate with those people. They are unveiling their faces. They are Israelites. They are making devourers of themselves by finding their inner eye.

Elisha uncovered Gehazi's eye for him enough once, so that to his amazement, he saw a host of defenders of Elisha encamped in the airs of the mountains round about Samaria. All the will of a king could not make an army seem strong enough to Elisha to hurt a hair of his head. All the will of the theology of Jericho and Gilgal combined could not veil Elisha's eye into seeing a cruse of oil as stopping because its quantum ordained by mathematical reason and good common sense had run out. (Verse 10) demonstrated.

The inner eye uncovered devours the wills of men as fast as they come near. It devours the performances called warfare, school teaching, temple building, buying and selling, marrying, manufacturing, dying, trying. He swalloweth up death in victory.

All the men who have unveiled their one inner eye, even if only partially, have been miracle workers. They showed other men by thousands exactly what they saw. Moses saw 2,000,000 slaves liberated without striking a blow. The slaves of our plantations were set free by a slight exhibition of this sight principle. They kept as still as death while we fell for them; but France fought man to man, slaying themselves for her freedom. The more the inner eye has been uncovered, the less violence there has been in devouring opposition. Hesekiah never lifted a finger to defend his city's freedom, but it cost 185,000 dead Assyrians. In devouring the wills of this age, instead of being devoured by them (Verse 5) we are to have no dead to mark our victories. *"Peace on earth; good will to men."*

Somebody saw in his mind's eye how it would look to be drawing millions of dollars out of his fellow-citizens' pockets, and he kept that will going till he got a hundred million. But the carrying out of that artificial will cost the underpaid toil of ten thousand half-grown girls. With them he wove cloth and built hospitals and public gardens, and we bowed our grateful heads to thank God for being devoured by this man's civilization. But that will of his had nothing whatsoever to do with the impartial will that liveth and dieth not wherein all that which ought to be is.

Our globe is now covered with those artificial wills. Be not devoured by them. Keep out of them, and *"I will rebuke the devourer for your sakes"*.

Whoever sees from the inner eyes keeps out of Samaria which is civilization, and out of gentile minds which formulate civilization. All who are setting forth to see the marvelous city of beauty which truly does lie near at hand, must know, to set out with, that the great Apollyon of time is artificial will.

Savonarola set up an imaginary city in the air. He held on firmly to imagining that city. (All our men who set out to bring things to pass have been noted for their firmness). When the old city built by the hard imaginations of his self-willed predecessors was besieged by some other strong-willed gentiles, Savonarola willed his imaginary city to stand still in the midst of the old terrified city then being besieged. It acted like magic. One event and then another transpired to make his imaginary city a defense to the besieged one. He was playing quick Gentilism. The city operations played Samaria.

Some Gentiles have strong magnetic forces. Things crackle and snap to their artificial determinations. Napoleon had a good stock of this. It usually breaks down and dissolves when a man is between 40 and 50 years of age. The conditions it has formulated still stand. The Gentile wills dissolve but Samaria remains. Some Gentiles have strong thought projectiles. They act like drivers' whips in a cotton field. Men and women, cities and systems snap and run at their artificially set-up models. Our great preachers, generals, kings were of this order. That breaks up somewhere about 60 in a man. Their systems and nations stay on, but well for the race that the men broke up, and well for the race when their systems and fatherlands are dissolved. For they were all wills that hid their neighbors' faces from sight of this kingdom that lies so close. (Verse 7)

The Message Heard By Matthew

No wonder Matthew heard the only one who saw into that kingdom where all that is was always as it is, say, *"I came not to do mine own will, but the will of him that sent me"*. He was showing me how to cease planting my imaginations in the midst of this people. He was telling the Greeks to stop whirling their systems before men's eyes. He

was telling the Generals, and Kings, and statesmen; he was telling stoics, gnostics, agnostics,
philosophers to cease their veiling palavers; for
something is. It is at hand; close by; it is an impar-
tially distributing giver. (Verse 8)

No matter where you go you will find some
people who are not altogether satisfied with the
way those who have been called the able men,
great men, bright men, rich men, have managed
this world's affairs. Those who are not pleased are
Israelites. They are not quite mesmerized to dead
automata. They have bolted. If even only slightly
dissatisfied, they are showing signs of trying to see
with the inner eye.

Go out independently, knowing that something
within you sees your way for you; call it the Jesus
Christ sight and plunge ahead. Talk of the kingdom all built. Talk with those who have not settled
down dumbly into admiration of the wills that
built up civilization. After awhile there is so much
talk of the kingdom that is — the kingdom wherein the tired mother's worn hands may rest and the
world-haggard father may revive — that those
great and wonderful men whom civilized cities
prostrate themselves before in profound admiration, those men who willed all the money their
minds could firmly gather in by killing men, or
over-working children, or any of the splendid modern ways, yea, even they will cease blowing dust
before the world's eyes and hear of it!

You will not need to take any money with you to hire people to hear about their own home. Ears will hearken, eyes will glisten, hearts will leap, when you tell of the city that lieth so close, whose maker and builder is God. Everywhere you go the best room will await you, the board will be spread. Only tell them of home. *"In my father's house there are many mansions."* (Verse 10)

The more you talk of this kingdom that lieth so close, the brighter your hopes will grow, your faith increases, the years speed on but the sweetness of your ministry fainteth not, but re-enforces itself with newer and newer elixirs. The dissatisfied are the first to listen. There are new ways of being housed and fed springing up wherever the kingdom that lieth so close is much talked of.

Every now and then we can hear a tongue that speaks as if it had licked from the altar fire of the home where no sorrow or poverty ever entered, but then its owner is devoured by civilized methods again, has entered Samaria; is not a devourer, but is devoured. His inner eye was not so nearly opened as we first thought. It was only another artificial will to hide the kingdom; not a ceasing of the will that the kingdom might be exposed.

The Note Which Shatters Walls Of Flesh

The dissatisfied are the most ready to hear of this city that nobody builded by making his neighbor toil, or beautified by the pain of even a bird. Those who feel that they must go along as the rest of the world is going are not to hear about the city till thousands and thousands have laid off the thoughts of sages, kings, philosophers, statesmen, generals. Then the air is so full of winds from the hill tops and valleys where the gateways are being opened that lead into its happy streets that they also will be glad to hear of home. (Verse 14)

The universal conspiracy against the rights of man is not defeatable by the combined efforts of the mission hearted of all the continents. Their efforts are only some more wills striking athwart the visions of mankind to hide just as densely as now this kingdom preached by Jesus Christ. One man alone with his eye single to its presence, without will, telling of it, seeing it closer and closer, is more of a devourer of misery than 10.000 together with an imagination of what they want done. "One shall put to flight 10,000." For he will gather in the Gentiles. He will swallow up death-dealing wills. He will sustain his one note on the walls of civilization till they crumble and fall; dissolved, together with the wills that built them.

Joshua sustained one bugle call until Jericho fell down. Matthew says that when the Jesus Christ in man speaks he sustains one note on the walls that hide this city so close at our hand till they fall and we are at home. At home in that city where all is finished and there is none to molest or make afraid.

The Jesus Christ note has been sustained so steadily now the kingdom not made of the will of flesh, but of God, has been so steadily told of that there is not much more fabric in the hiding veils — those walls built of powerful imaginations stand firm, steadfast generals of human destiny.

The new race of the single eye, the new tongue that tells of the one impartial will, the Jesus Christ type of man is here. He is apparently a sheep in the midst of wolves, but the nations will soon discover that he has devoured the death which they instituted, the unequal distribution of opportunities which their policies have fashioned, the squalor and shame and pain of civilization. He will lift up the heads of those who have been taking as God's will our human destiny, fashioned by the firm wills of what we have called our great men while pulling and shaping things and men and systems to do their will. He who preaches of the kingdom so nigh at hand sees it; seeing it, his eye is single to it, and single-eyed to it he brings the devouring fire of the end of time with his heaven-lit glance over kingdoms, principalities, philosophies, and their builders.

Inter-Ocean Newspaper December 16, 1894

LESSON XII

Unto Us A Child Is Born

Luke 7:24-35, Isaiah 9:3-7

The great musician's eyes seem always to be looking backward and upward. He also has stumbled upon the first lesson of Jesus Christ. The great artist's eyes have an upward and backward expression, as though he saw into some exalted region of his own being. He also is stumbling toward doing that which Jesus of Nazareth said was a miracle-working principle.

We hear a great deal about getting one's self into harmony with certain forces that are supposed to be moving through this universe. We are told that there is a secret "glame" (old term for reflected ice crystals in the atmosphere) in our atmospheric ether which we can extract after a little practice and it will have an astonishing effect upon us. We are told of elixirs that float and crackle all about us, which only a few on this round ball have ever caught any of, but they have been filled with extraordinary powers.

According to Jesus Christ those powers really all start from the soul principle in each one of us, and it is what we ourselves have generated that we finally inhale as "glame", *"elixir vitae"*, or "forces".

"The kingdom of heaven cometh not by observation" of the outside world. As long as we look that way we shall see the prison face the church and the poorhouse glare at the college. The first lesson of Jesus was, "Stop gazing among the ways of men hoping to find a cure of their scourges. Turn your eyes backward and see into that kingdom of heaven that hath its everlasting abode within you. There your eyes will catch fire, light, miracle shining rays, and wherever you look after that something new and strange will happen."

"The kingdom of heaven is within you. Behold! Heal the sick, cast out devils, raise the dead. These signs shall follow."

He taught that, standing at the belt line between reality and unreality, we will take our choice; look at soul or not soul. The soul is that deep place in man that says "God is". There are no outward signs of any God such as man proclaims. He always insists when he speaks from his soul that God is good, but there are more signs that the ruling principle is evil than good. There are five times as many words to express evil as to express good, and five times as many signs of evil as good. But such signs all come from "without" where dogs and sorcerers and whatsoever makath and loveth lies.

The first thing to do in order to be natural, as we stand here at this belt line between the without and the within, is to keep a steady eye on the soul. When the dogs and sorcerers and lies will dissolve into nowhere. This turning back of the vision faculty is the mystic meaning of "repentance".

In The Light That Is Within

Whoever, in the deeps of mental darkness, sorrow disappointment, keeps for a certain stretch of time his vision fixed on his own soul, suddenly, sometimes catches the fact that there is a mysterious light, different from sunlight, different from electricity, different from any light he has ever seen, which is in himself, around himself. He becomes aware of being a different being; from what he was before. Looking around he finds very few, if any, of his neighbors shining with that quality. Under these circumstances he must be thoroughly acquainted with some of the principles, the letters, which that light faithfully watched and rightly named has revealed to unmistakably truthful people, or he will get to speaking very hatefully of his neighbors because they do not have that light he has exposed.

Then he will get the name of being a great religionist. He will scold and lash and condemn those who are going back over the tracks toward their soul by scientific statements. But they, poor things, are traveling as best they know to that region from whence he let loose the light. He says they are not spiritual, they are intellectual they devote too much time to scientific reasonings.

But when that light does break through and over those who have been very obediently reasonable in their statements, they will know better than to scold and lash other people for keeping the letter of the truth long before they see the light thereof.

As the "glame" which people catch in the atmosphere is really something which they liberated from within themselves, so the light which is caught stealing out from watching our own soul is what we liberate. The musician turned back toward his inner kingdom and liberated harmony. The healer turned back to his own soul kingdom and liberated soul health. Each one wonders why the other does not liberate his particular genius.

Today's lesson has for its principal theme: "Unto us a child is born". We have liberated something. Each one has borne from within, outward, some new genius. What is it? If it is born from the very altar fire of the heaven within ourselves, through steadfast watching it according to the mystic direction of Jesus, it here declares that *"of its increase there shall be no end."* (Isaiah 9:7)

If it is born from looking away from our own soul we are told that we may indeed have multiplied, but no joy comes with it. (Isaiah 9:3) There is no forgiveness without repentance. That is, we have no streaming forth of enduring power, light, heavenly miracles, except from first finding the deep place within us which not only says, "God is," but knows it. Then, finding it, we must "watch" — watch till the light breaks forth. Watching is repentance — turning back, retracing steps. Streaming light of any kind is forgiveness.

Significance Of The Vision Of Isaiah

The artist sees beautiful colors everywhere. This is the nature of his liberated vision. The musician hears tones everywhere. This is his kind of forgiveness — giving for. The sorrowful one sees the finger of God everywhere. When they, any of them, begin to find flaws and inharmonies they shut the gates again. They must strike back toward the soul point again. *"For always without are dogs,"* said Jesus till you have really struck your vision like grappling hooks back and up into the exalted heaven. *"Therefore turn ye."*

Isaiah looked by prophetic glance into our day, and there he saw us as a people wandering in very great darkness of trouble of all sorts. He saw that though a great separating of good from evil, reality from unreality, disease from health, had been made by pronouncing health the supreme over sickness, and reality the supreme over unreality, yet the world was fairly anguishing with hate.

Isaiah had looked backward toward the soul kingdom by some process of thinking which had liberated prophetic knowledge for him. Paul called it the "gift of prophecy". He flung forward his searchlight into our own age and there he finds us, A.D. 1894, with nearly every sentient creature wise enough to discriminate between good and evil, spirit and matter, Christ principles and world methods, and yet this discrimination knowledge not lessening but rather intensifying the hatred of life conditions.

So it is Isaiah's privilege, as well as Daniel's and the revelator's, to find a wonderful light breaking out and shining around about this time. Not the light of distinguishing between good and evil; that light was the separator's light. Not the light of knowing the Christ principles of daily conduct; that light is the separator's light. Not the light of knowing the way to reason on the side of spirit till spirit sets material conditions face to face with you, while the whole spiritual reasoning rests like a splendid globe of inactivity just as visible; that is the winnower's light. That is the judgment hour.

It is, rather, the arrival of a new light with power in itself to do what none of the other lights have accomplished. The man who finds so much evil in me is looking with one eye over the belt line among the husks of unreality, while with the other he knows what I ought to be. This is not a joyous light. It makes him miserable to see such a discrepancy, and it makes me miserable to be cast in with the goats by his mind. "This is not that light" that is to break forth about this time. This is not the child to be born to this hour for the whole world.

Signs of The Times

We are living, as Isaiah and Daniel saw us, in a time when all the people on the planet know and think, dress and sing, eat and study, about the same things. Differences of color, climate, ancestry, counts now for little or nothing. Therefore, that which happens must be a world event. (Verse 7)

The time of social distinctions is closing. The time of settings up and puttings down is ending. The time when I am rich and you are poor is arrested. The time when by some secret contrivance I can be defamed or defended by anybody that lives is finished. This is not only true of one person, individual, identity, but of all. *"This shall be with burning and with fuel of fire."* (Verse 5)

Whoever sees the starting signals of this light is so busy watching it, that he is not interested in my wickedness enough even to pray over it. The redeeming light absorbs all his vision. Whoever sees this star, whose flash on the belt line of time dazzles the mind with a new effulgence, when it is discovered to be the long anticipated sun, sees that all his piety is nothing — nothing; as nothing as my wickedness. He sees that, "the righteousness of the righteous does not save him nor the wickedness of the wicked destroy him," for the whole earth burneth as an oven under the new light.

Isaiah was lighting his eyes backward at the altar fire of his heaven within, exactly as the artist lights his eyes backward at the heavenly mount within himself; and Isaiah threw forward his sights on the canvas of time exactly as the artist throws forward his sights on the canvas of cloth.

Other men watch the artist's vision and call it inspiration. Other men watch the prophet's vision and call it inspiration. The closer their grappling irons struck into the kingdom that is not alterable, the more enduring their paintings. Isaiah's painting is still quivering with vitality after twenty-six hundred years of expression. The divine Raphael's visions still make beholders weep with touches of far-off but deathless memories of heaven.

But in this day all men, are to find their minds simultaneously turning backward to their own soul. They shall, as one man, watch it steadfastly. They shall not face the life conditions they hate so hard nor face the spiritual reasonings that have explained those conditions as phantoms of nothingness. They shall watch their own soul. And unto them a new and glorious morning breaks.

"O, earth! Where is thy stinging darkness, when morn of heaven shines on my life? O, religion, where is thy unfulfilling promise when the true God is sighted by my repenting vision?"

The New Born Story Of God

Thus shall a whole world sing. Not one left out. All telling the same story. Not good, not evil, but the new born story. It breaks the yoke of all men's burdens. It takes the staff of religion off man's stooping shoulders. It takes off the rod of mind with its perpetual reasonings that whirl and whirl on the same axis time in and time out, so that we find ourselves today not a whit ahead of Chinese speculative philosophy of a thousand years B.C. It settles all the confusions of multitudinous sciences. It ends the competitions of man with man which have rolled his garments in the blood of crying beasts and unpitied toilers. (Verses 4, 5)

Religion could not do this. Philosophy has failed. Civilization has only added confusion to confusion. So the mind of man now turns back-ward and simultaneously stares at his own soul. This is repenting. There we find "the city whose builder and maker is God." We see face to face the countenance of a new power. This new power has a name. Isaiah called it "wonderful," "Counselor," "mighty God." John the Revelator called it "Jesus Christ." Daniel called it "Michael." But all have united in calling it "Light."

We are repenting as a world. Mark that! Turn-ing back from watching the imaginary notions of men, which are all that the best of our religions and the best of our sciences amount to, and noting that the kingdom of heaven lieth foursquare in its beauty within our own selves every one. No man so sinful but his backward turning vision can kin-dle at the fires of his own soul's heaven, and make him see heaven everywhere. No man so poor but his backward turning vision may kindle at the hearth fire of his own soul's home and show him God's impartial plenty everywhere.

Immaculate Vision Impossible To None

Immaculate vision is possible in the most out-wardly depraved. As Mary of Bethlehem caught immaculate vision of the kingdom of Heaven where her soul was dwelling, so all women, all men may catch immaculate vision of their un-stainable soul.

As Mary of Bethlehem brought forth Jesus, the matchless; as his vision brought forth the God in the fishermen; as the vision brought forth a new era, so all mankind's united vision of their own soul kingdom, doth bring the new heaven and new earth everywhere.

"And now it shall be, saith the shining Lord, that thou shalt call me Ishi; and shalt call me no more Baal". (Hosea 2:16) Thou shalt be entered into thy inheritance. Thou shalt not be waiting and hoping for thy light; it is come unto thee, and none shall be afraid again for evermore. For the Lord that the world seeth hath done great and mighty and glad things. The true light is shining. The very islands of the sea feel it beams. The mountains of the west catch its healing changes. The new age opens with the unprecedented situation of every human being's now looking backward into his own soul's kingdom and loosening his attention from the grip of his neighbor's imaginary religion, science or philosophy.

Inter-Ocean Newspaper December 23, 1894

LESSON XIII

Review

Isaiah 9:2-7

There are three planes of interpretation upon which to speak or write all the texts of the world's Bibles and the world's experiences. There is;

First, the literal. "The letter killeth."

Second, the metaphysical or ideal. "The kingdom of God is not in idea." Third, the absolute. "Yesterday, today, and forever," the same unalterable state. (Heb13:8)

We take such a text as this one, for example: "Yet a little sleep, a little slumber, a little folding of the hands to sleep; so shall thy poverty come as one that traveleth and thy want as an armed man". On the literal plane we were routed up at 4 o'clock mornings to be on hand at the workshop or stockyards, lest by a trifle more sleep each morning we should he numbered among the paupers.

On the metaphysical plane we were instructed never to let the mind droop back into old thoughts, as that death is reality or sickness is a substance, lest we should find the true ideas departed from us and we be poorer off than before we knew that nature is but a mirror of thoughts.

On the absolute plane we know that the kingdom into which we are privileged to look was always what it is, and neither sleep nor sheep killing performed by me can alter it or its relations to us. It has only one lesson or direction forever, and that is: "Turn Ye". Jesus called it "repent". He had no reference to wickedness. He well knew that if my eyes are glued to planting corn or setting type as my way of getting life, there is nothing but voluntary ungluing that will show me any other way. By his one lesson hammered on for three years by him. I find that the least bit of sleep, slumber, non-observance of world methods on my part will bring me into sight of heaven, where the poverty of Sons of God is their glorious freedom from the luggage of chair and clothes, ideas and sciences.

The kingdom of heaven is a country on this side the belt-line of vision. We all belong in it. We are there absolutely uncumbered by things or thoughts. This is the poverty of the absolute. The

power of one glance backward is beyond description. "An armed man" is the synonym of power.
Thy want of sight of things and thoughts is purest
want. "The pure see God." By seeing anything we
become it.

"For what thou seest, man,

   That, too, become thou must.

God, if thou seest God,

   Dust, if thou seest dust."

That Which Will Be Found In The Kingdom

What powers fling their splendors forward on
the desert marches of humanity when we sleep a
second from observation of world gymnastics and
philosophic gyrations?

The blind received their sight, and we have the
gospel that causes the beggar woman to share and
share alike with Gabriel.

They do not have to think and think in the
kingdom that lieth back of us all in order to keep
sickness from paralyzing their fingers. They think
not. And, oh, they do not have to follow the whispering religions of a Calvin or a Buddha in order
to find their homes in heaven, and keep them forever and ever. They agree with nothing and
nobody. "They neither marry nor are given in marriage." All agreement is a species of marriage.

They agree not in heaven. The soul within man never yet agreed with anything. It is glued to nothing. "Watch it." Softly, noiselessly, in such an hour as ye think not, in such an hour as ye sleep, slumber, from agreeing with Franklin on the "work or starve" theory; or agree with metaphysics on the "think or die" theory, thy soul standeth forth strong as an armed man, and its kingdom shines far on the hills and valleys of earth, finding on its gleaming pathway no more pain, neither sorrow nor starving.

Every religion is a species of thinking out from a premise. It was somebody's fad, originally, and it glued many multitudes to its lingo. But Jesus Christ has nothing to do with religion. That is, the soul in man never was glued, never agreed, never married. The golden text of today, selected by the world's committee, declares that what it was it is, and it forever will be, independent of any man's reasonings.

Every philosophy is a species of thinking out from a premise. It was somebody's fad, originally, and it glued many or few to its lingo. Every science is likewise a whirring and tiresome fad. It has nothing whatsoever to do with the Jesus Christ or soul in man. It may please the intellect to leap from limb to limb of splendid logic on the subject of God and no God, on the subject of interetheric forces and ratios of sunbeams, but the soul never thinks, never reasons, never wills; takes no interest in science, religion, or philosophy, for all these daze and tire, and each age laughs at the former for believing in them.

The one lesson of the Galilean, whose vision always struck healing glory on the crouching victims of religion and science, was "Watch!" Take close note of him. He shed his watch rays on the stars of the aged skies and they darkened. His closing eyelids hid the everlasting sun. His loud word cracked the tombs of time, and men came up to walk again among the changeless hills and trees of beautiful Jerusalem. Take note of him because he said he had nothing to do with this world, where principles clash and clatter. "My kingdom is not of this world."

Situation of Time And Religion Reviewed

He took death on his shoulders and let it fall off again. He took pain in his fingers and let it fall down. He took disgrace, spitting, mocking, and let them drop down. They touched not his unidentified being. Take note of him; untaught of books, and listless when preachers in fine broadcloth shout their hypnotizing explanations. Take note of him, for he said: "I have my eternal abode in you, and there is where you will find me."

Observe not what the sciences are claiming. Observe not the crime and goodness of mankind. "The kingdom of heaven cometh not by observation." "Look unto me." "I stand at the door." "My name is charged with heaven as Plato's is charged with philosophy." "The green hills that never heard a cry, the amethystine shadows that fling long their smiling streams from valley to valley where no trouble ever walked, are my place of abode within the drunken sailor and the puritan maiden are one and the same."

"The kingdom of heaven is in you, everyone. One look is enough.   One look is repentance enough."

This being the last Sunday of 1894, the subject is "Review". If we review the situations of time and religion from observation we make one set of statements. These statements have no heavenly power in them. If we review the situations of time end religion from the other standpoint we are lifted out of all observable realms and put by one swing of the absolute out off the touch of things and thoughts.

Observed by the standard of discriminative judgment, discriminative prejudices, we see that since Christian Science flung her banner on the winds of human mind poverty has multiplied and replenished, war has focalized her cruelties, the rich have swollen richer, and the poor have gaunted poorer.

If rum and whiskey have multiplied their bar-
rels since temperance women set up their
platforms, so have trouble and terror multiplied
their appearances since Christian Science set up
their pulpits

Plea That Judgment May Be Righteous

The war cry that spirit is all, matter is nothing, has rolled materially into one great globe in
plain sight of all eyes, and rolled spiritual reasonings into another great globe facing material
conditions, but not dissolving them.

Be fair. In reviewing situations apply one cru-
cial test to all the whirring systems gluing the
attentions of men.

There where Oriental Metaphysics sheds her
white beams across the Thibetan plains, how dissolving are they of matter's tattered millions?
Here where science sheds her electric gleams from
mountain-topped Christianity how dissolving are
they of saddening matter's grip on the efforts of
this multitude?

What now? This is the judgment hour. Let
matter's globe, with all the inhabitants thereof,
keep at it. Let them alone. "He that is filthy, let
him be filthy still." They have silently moved into
their places of their own accord. Can you turn the
man who deals with matter into any interest out-

side bread and fish and the study of dried bones, or accounts and machines?

Can you turn the man who deals with thoughts into any interest outside the power and prowess of his own system of religion or philosophy? "He that is righteous let him be righteous still."

This is one kind of review. It exhibits in all its bold bad facts the impotence of religion, science, art, education, to touch with anything but the separator's fan the conditions of the world. And it brings to its bold absolute the assertion of the soul in man that knows not matter; never was enlisted while he slew with outward hands herds of men or beasts; never was enlisted in the religion the mental hands of him swung round and round and up and down; knows nothing of that gorgeous opposite to matter called spirit; is poor in spirit, and being neither spirit nor matter it walks its majestic nature safely between them.

The Souls Of All One And Changeless

These opposites fall into the risen light and are never heard of anymore. Death is swallowed up of victory, and all her workers likewise. Life is swallowed up of victory and all his reasoners with him. "There is one Lord and his name one." What is this? It is that one within all alike. It never reviews past systems or future worlds. There is no time to it; there are no kingdoms but its kingdom to it.

As the mental gaze is turned to watch your own soul all your mind falls into its un-mindedness. All your bodily frame drops in likewise. But though you fall you rise. Though you are lost you are found. You are now yourself.

"It is decreed that earth,

From this time ever forth,

Shall, rise and ever rise

Through all eternities."

So sleep and slumber are godlike when interpreted, not from observation of mental operations of physical panoramas, but from the soul standard. They mean non-observation of flesh. "The flesh profiteth nothing." They mean non-observation of thoughts. "In such an hour as ye think not."

So want and poverty are divine states when interpreted from the non-observable side. So power is a quality that streams through the open doorway made by the ever present faculty of vision turned backward toward the kingdom of heaven within each one alike.

There is no trying to do miracles. They are obliged to follow watching the soul. "These signs shall follow."

Literal and physical interpretations of situations are judgments from observation. They have no heaven in them. Metaphysical interpretations are likewise judgments from observation. They have no heaven in them. The absolute interpretation is forecast of the language of heaven. It calls attention to the kingdom within Sullivan, St. John, and myself, one the same changeless thing, whose last and most dissolving name gospel and revelator unite in telling me how to pronounce, that heaven in all its tinting happy hues may gleam on the rooftrees of a home alike for Guiteau and Jesus, the beggar and me.

Inter-Ocean Newspaper December 30, 1894

Notes

Other Books by Emma Curtis Hopkins

- *Class Lessons of 1888 (WiseWoman Press)*
- *Bible Interpretations (WiseWoman Press)*
- *Esoteric Philosophy in Spiritual Science (WiseWoman Press)*
- *Genesis Series*
- *High Mysticism (WiseWoman Press)*
- *Self Treatments with Radiant I Am (WiseWoman Press)*
- *Gospel Series (WiseWoman Press)*
- *Judgment Series in Spiritual Science (WiseWoman Press)*
- *Drops of Gold (WiseWoman Press)*
- *Resume (WiseWoman Press)*
- *Scientific Christian Mental Practice (DeVorss)*

Books about Emma Curtis Hopkins and her teachings

- *Emma Curtis Hopkins, Forgotten Founder of New Thought –* Gail Harley
- *Unveiling Your Hidden Power: Emma Curtis Hopkins' Metaphysics for the 21st Century (also as a Workbook and as A Guide for Teachers) – Ruth L. Miller*
- *Power to Heal: Easy reading biography for all ages –Ruth Miller*

To find more of Emma's work, including some previously unpublished material, log on to:

www.highwatch.org
www.emmacurtishopkins.com

WISEWOMAN PRESS

Books Published by WiseWoman Press

By Emma Curtis Hopkins

- *Resume*
- *Gospel Series*
- *Class Lessons of 1888*
- *Self Treatments including Radiant I Am*
- *High Mysticism*
- *Esoteric Philosophy in Spiritual Science*
- *Drops of Gold Journal*
- *Judgment Series*
- *Bible Interpretations: series I, thru XIV*

By Ruth L. Miller

- *Unveiling Your Hidden Power: Emma Curtis Hopkins' Metaphysics for the 21st Century*
- *Coming into Freedom: Emily Cady's Lessons in Truth for the 21st Century*
- *150 Years of Healing: The Founders and Science of New Thought*
- *Power Beyond Magic: Ernest Holmes Biography*
- *Power to Heal: Emma Curtis Hopkins Biography*
- *The Power of Unity: Charles Fillmore Biography*
- *Power of Thought: Phineas P. Quimby Biography*
- *Gracie's Adventures with God*
- *Uncommon Prayer*
- *Spiritual Success*
- *Finding the Path*

www.wisewomanpress.com

List of
Bible Interpretation Series

with date from 1st to 14th Series.

This list is complete through the fourteenth Series. Emma produced at least thirty Series of Bible Interpretations.

She followed the Bible Passages provided by the International Committee of Clerics who produced the Bible Quotations for each year's use in churches all over the world.

Emma used these for her column of Bible Interpretations in both the Christian Science Magazine, at her Seminary and in the Chicago Inter-Ocean Newspaper.

First Series

155

Second Series

Third Series

Fourth Series

Fifth Series

Sixth Series

Seventh Series

Eighth Series

Ninth Series

165

Tenth Series

Eleventh Series

169

Twelfth Series

171

Thirteenth Series

July 1 – September 30, 1894

Lesson 1	The Birth of Jesus	July 1st
	Luke 2:1-16	
	No Room for Jesus	
	Man's Mystic Center	
	They glorify their Performances	
Lesson 2	Presentation in the Temple	July 8th
	Luke 2:25-38	
	A Light for Every Man	
	All Things Are Revealed	
	The Coming Power	
	Like the Noonday Sun	
Lesson 3	Visit of the Wise Men	July 15th
	Matthew 1:2-12	
	The Law Our Teacher	
	Take neither Scrip nor Purse	
	The Star in the East	
	The Influence of Truth	
Lesson 4	Flight Into Egypt	July 22nd
	Mathew 2:13-23	
	The Magic Word of Wage Earning	
	How Knowledge Affect the Times	
	The Awakening of the Common People	
Lesson 5	The Youth of Jesus	July 29th
	Luke2:40-52	
	Your Righteousness is as filthy Rags	
	Whatsoever Ye Search, that will Ye Find	
	The starting Point of All Men	
	Equal Division, the Lesson Taught by Jesus	
	The True Heart Never Falters	
Lesson 6	The "All is God" Doctrine	August 5th
	Luke 2:40-52	
	Three Designated Stages of Spiritual Science	
	Christ Alone Gives Freedom	
	The Great Leaders of Strikes	
Lesson 7	Missing	August 12th
Lesson 8	First Disciples of Jesus	August 19th
	John 1:36-49	
	The Meaning of Repentance	

172

173

Fourteenth Series

Made in the USA
Lexington, KY
20 May 2012